Rooftop Perspectives

Rooftop Perspectives

DISCIPLE YOUR STUDENTS TOWARD FAITH
DEVELOP THEIR LOVE FOR WISDOM
AND CUT THE PUPPET'S STRINGS

Eric Reenders

Eric Reenders
www.rooftopperspectives.com
email: eric@rooftopperspectives.com

Book Layout ©2013 BookDesignTemplates.com
Cover design by Michelle Lovi
www.odysseybooks.com.au
Cover photo by Bo Wen Chin

Rooftop Perspectives/ Eric Reenders —1st ed.
ISBN-13: 978-0615918617
ISBN-10: 0615918611

Dedication

To my partner in educating those most dear to us – my wonderful, inspirational wife, Christie, to those most precious students, my Rebecca and Jadelin, and to all the fantastic teachers I have met, worked with, and learned from, over the years who love their students... and want to spend eternity with them.

Contents

INTRODUCTION

Nothing short of a great Civil War of Values rages today throughout North America. Two sides with vastly differing and incompatible world-views are locked in a bitter conflict that permeates every level of society. ... Instead of fighting for territory or military conquest, however, the struggle now is for the hearts and minds of the people. It is a war over ideas. And, someday soon, I believe, a winner will emerge and the loser will fade from memory. ... As we will see, the hottest battles in this civil war are being fought on educational turf, and this is where eventual victory or defeat will occur. *

Dr. James Dobson

Dr. Dobson wrote those prophetic words over 20 years ago... today we see proof that he was correct every time we turn on the television or log into the internet, proof that we are indeed loosing the battle on many fronts. Ultimately, I believe we will win the war. Our God is stronger. We have confidence we are on the winning side. This confidence unfortunately can have a downside. When victory is assured it's easy to say the occasional battle lost doesn't matter all that much. However, in war, each lost battle has casualties... and in this case, the casualties are eternal. These casualties are our students and as Christian teachers we will one day have to answer for them.

History shows, those with a united front, a united focus, are far more likely to prevail. So too, we as believers, working in education, engaged in the front lines of the battle, need a united focus. I believe that is what this new paradigm I have to share with you will offer.

I didn't write this book in the conventional way of education literature. I believe that by the end you will understand why. I believe you will be entertained, enlighte·ned and encouraged and, in the end, it will give you the tools you need to start changing the course of the battle for your students. I believe that working together with a shared focus, by the grace of God, victory is at hand. I hope you will join the conversation. Let's stand shoulder to shoulder on the front-line. ... Here is the battleplan...

*James C. Dobson and Gary L. Bauer, *Children at Risk: The Battle for the Hearts and Minds of Our Kids* (Dallas: Word Publishing, 1990), 19, 37.

Part one

ONE

At the moment the only thought going through John's head was, "How on earth does a place that gets as hot as this one does in the summer ever get this stinking cold?" Everywhere he looked everything was frozen solid and had been for more than a month yet there was no snow whatsoever. It was so cold even the dry air itself seemed to have taken on a bluish tint which seemed to blanch the color out of everything. The thought that would have next jumped unbidden to John's mind would have been "What on earth am I doing here?" but it died a premature death as a strong gust of the ever-present wind pushed its way through his parka making him snug up his scarf and push on against the gale.

John stepped off the curb and nearly fell when he slipped on, well he wasn't sure what he slipped on. He really didn't want to think about it in this land where one had to be so careful of what one steps on. For that matter, right now, thinking was something he really wanted to avoid, there had been too much of it already. Thought. Pointless. The cold was a blessing forcing his mind further inward, beyond thought to the place most focused with survival, a surprisingly peaceful place.

He gingerly, with a touch more survival focus, made his way across the street and turned left into a previously unexplored part of this sprawling village of twelve million. For what many would call a third world nation this one surely had prospered since the first time he had visited just more than ten years prior. He consciously decided not to think about the twists and turns his life had taken since that first visit, ultimately leading him and his family to live in this weather forsaken place. The whole point of being out braving the twenty-degrees-below-freezing temperature and the ridiculous wind was to clear his head, to not think. Don't think. Impossible. "At least think about something different," he told himself.

Continuing up the street he forced his eyes up from the buckled and broken pavers of the sidewalk with its deadly patches of frozen filth and began to really focus on his surroundings. He was on one of the smaller old streets that in the summer would be quite charming with its old brick buildings and the solid canopy of trees shading everything. Children would be playing. Old men would be squatting around low tables on even lower stools playing mahjong and laughing over their tea. Cicadas would be buzzing in the trees, a warm cacophony of noise and life. Now, the trees were bare. Everything was frozen and blue tinged and dirty. Sounds were sharp and brittle.

There was hardly a person in sight as on a day like this. The only people who would be outside were those who had to be. This suited John just fine. Today he didn't want to talk. Didn't want to struggle through the answers to all the standard questions. "Where are you from? How long have you been here? What do you do?" He just wanted to walk. To walk in the cold and not think. Don't think. He focused on the numerous small shops fronting the buildings and tried in vain to make some sense of the innumerable signs but there was no use. He was certain one day he would be able to master the multiple tones of the local language but he had no such hope of ever being able to read. He was fairly certain that the written language was based on the tracks of a one-legged chicken scratching for its next meal. Incomprehensible.

"What kind of mind thought that one up?" he wondered. "And I thought I had problems," he laughed darkly.

John continued on, braced against the cold and, for the most part succeeded in not thinking. So lost was he in his own non-thoughts that he was taken aback for a moment when he finally realized that he had stopped walking and was instead staring at a sign above a dingy open doorway that lead to a flight of bare cement stairs extending up into darkness. It took him a moment to realize that he could actually read the sign. That was rare indeed. As he tried to decipher just what a "LiuPing Cafe" was, he came to another startling revelation. Someone was talking to him.

John squinted to make out the source of the nasal, high pitched, rapid fire voice coming at him from the shadow of the doorway but it was no use. The contrast of the darkness of the stairwell and the blinding blue light outside was too great for his eyes to adjust to. As the voice continued on John shook his head and mumbled, "ting bu dong." I hear you but I don't understand, a fairly standard conversation ender for him. As he turned to move on laughter erupted from the shadows and a figure stepped out into the light.

"You crazy American. I'm speaking English. Don't you understand your own language? You've been in cold too long," the figure laughed.

John just stood there staring while he inwardly laughed because this guy sounded just like the duck that sold noodles in the panda movie his kids loved to watch.

"What's the matter American, your tongue as frozen as your ears?"

"How do you know I'm American?" John asked dumbly.

More laughter. "How do you know a fish is a fish? Of course you are American." The figure smiled. "I live in America thirty years, California. Own two restaurant there. Very successful! I move back here, share what I learn there! I know American when I see one."

John looked at this stranger a little closer. He was about John's height and thin. He looked to be about fifty but John was terrible about guessing ages. The man's thin jet black hair was combed into an elaborate wave in a failed attempt to cover his bald spot. He seemed friendly enough but, two successful restaurants in California? If that were true what's he doing in this dump?

"I'm from California." John stammered a little off balanced from the whole thing, or, maybe it was just the cold getting to him.

"Yes, I figured," the man said, "only someone from warm place like California dumb enough to be out walking in this weather. You catch cold!"

More laughter. John decided that as friendly as this guy was he was getting tired of being laughed at. His mind was starting to turn back from the solitude of survival mode to the realm of thought and that just wouldn't do. He turned to go.

"Hey California, where you going? You need to take rest. Warm up. Drink something hot." A big smile. "You come to my cafe, I fix you right up!"

"Your cafe?"

"Yes, my cafe of course! My name LiuPing. My cafe just up these stairs. You come. I fix you right up!"

"So that explains it," thought John. "This guy's not so friendly he's just looking for business. Two restaurants in California, right..."

"Not today, I don't have any money with me," John lied and turned to go.

"No you come now!" LiuPing argued. "This is not business deal, cafe closed today. This is act of mercy. You freezing... can't even think straight."

"That's kind of the point," John thought.

"You don't even recognize English."

"He has a point." John considered. He really didn't want to see what kind of dump was at the top of those stairs though.

"I make special drink for you. Warm your body. Clear your mind! Very healthy!"

John relented, clearing his mind sounded perfect. "Ok, let's get out of the cold." As John stepped through the doorway and started to follow LiuPing up the dilapidated stairs he had the fleeting realization that whatever was at the top might not be any warmer than it was outside.

TWO

John wasn't sure what he had expected to find when they reached the cafe at the top of the stairs but the reality of it left him dumbfounded. What he noticed first as he came through the door was the incredible warmth of the place. It wasn't just the temperature which was nearly perfect. It was everything about the place from the polished wood floors, the light filtering through the thin, sheer, canvas window shades, to the wood paneled walls. Everything was warm and bright. Not the scorching blue bright of the frozen world outside but the soft filtered brightness of a late spring day. The kind of day where a breeze comes through the open window, ruffling the curtains, the diffused light casting shadows and prisms, and you just can't fight the urge to sink down into the covers of the bed and nap the afternoon away. That's exactly what John wanted to do right now, curl up in a warm sunny spot and nap. He, until that moment, hadn't realized just how tired he was.

"Welcome, welcome! Well don't just stand there. You're not that frozen," LiuPing laughed. "Take off your coat and stay awhile! I make you special drink from my hometown. Not even on the menu!"

John slipped the noose of his scarf and shrugged out of his parka like a butterfly emerging from its long sleep, the warmth washing over him. He glanced around the room for the best place to sit. There were low tables and couches, overstuffed armchairs with small wooden side tables between them. There were even a couple of what looked like family dinner tables made of very old lumber. John sunk down into the embrace of one of the armchairs and continued to survey the cafe.

John saw they weren't just on the top floor but above that, on the level of the rooftop. One wall had sliding glass doors that opened out onto a large patio. Actually, by the number of pots and the several large frozen trees, he thought it was probably, in more temperate seasons, a rooftop garden. Right now though, it was frozen and just the thought of going back out there made him shiver.

Turning his attention back inside he noticed the numerous bookshelves along the walls were filled with an astonishing number of books many of which had English titles. The shelves also held an array of curios he hadn't seen since California. There were model World War II biplanes, decorative coffee cups, handmade dolls and wooden toys, trinkets and baubles. All very tastefully arranged. Many of the walls had very well painted canvases, mostly of outdoor scenes, hung without frames. It seemed that there were things almost everywhere but nothing was overpowering. Everything was somehow perfectly balanced.

There was something else just pulling at the edges of his consciousness. Something there that he was missing. He scanned the room again to no avail but something was prickling his senses. Suddenly it hit him. Green! Living green. Chlorophyll. Plants. They were everywhere. On the bookshelves, on the tables, hanging from the ceiling in front of the windows, almost everywhere John looked there was something alive and green and thriving. John struggled to remember just how long it had been since he had seen a living, not frozen, plant. "Far too long!" he thought. What an amazing place this cafe was!

John looked across to where the proprietor was busying himself behind an immaculate wood and brass bar. Along the wall was a huge, ancient-looking, brass and copper espresso machine, a matching hand-cranked coffee grinder and alongside that, what looked like a coffee bean roaster. "He roasts his own beans," John chuckled to himself. "I'm so glad I decided to come in here!" On a shelf above were lined row after row of sparkling glasses, cups, and mugs. LiuPing wasn't using any of it. Instead, he had an old dented copper pot filled with water heating over a portable butane burner. As John watched, LiuPing took a huge piece of what looked like a plump yellow root, whacked it with the flat side of a massive cleaver, chopped it into several pieces and added it to the pot. He then poured in at least a cup of sugar and gave it a quick stir.

LiuPing noticed John watching. "You wonder what kind of crazy thing I make you drink eh?"

"Well, I was a bit curious. I can't say I've seen anyone make anything like it."

"This very popular drink when I was child. My grandmother taught me to make it. It is very ancient drink." LiuPing smiled. "Very good for you on cold day! You will like it!"

"With that awesome espresso machine I was kind of hoping for a cup of coffee," John said tentatively.

LiuPing laughed, "You think you know what you need. Ha ha, you not even smart enough to get out of the cold, almost frozen. You let LiuPing take care of you. You will like it! Fix you right up! Be ready in five minutes, that's all!"

"But, what is it?" John asked feeling more than a bit indignant. He knew exactly what he needed no matter what this crackpot thought. He leaned forward, elbows on his knees, chin resting on one fist.

"So many question you ask. They're not even the right questions. If you must have answers to everything you never be satisfied!"

"Not the right questions? I just want to know what you're making."

LiuPing smiled and came from behind the bar to take the armchair next to John. "Be patient and you will have your answers. I'm not going to poison you! Just a few minutes more and you will see."

John settled back into the embrace of the chair. His answers would have to wait... Like so many others in his life right now.

"So California, what's bothering you so much?"

John just stared at LiuPing and thought, "Is this guy psychic?"

LiuPing laughed again. "Maybe that question's too hard for your frozen brain California," he smiled. "Maybe easy question first?"

John, again feeling a bit miffed, nodded his assent.

"Ok, we start easy California. What is your name?"

"John."

"Oh, see, very easy! You answer right away!" LiuPing's smile made the room even warmer and John began to realize that maybe this strange character was just trying to cheer him up a bit. He smiled back despite himself and chuckled.

"See, I think you starting to warm up a bit. Maybe a bit harder question?"

John nodded.

"Why are you here?

John stared, stuttered. "Well, I've been under a ton of stress, too much to do and way too much to think about. So, I decided to go for a walk and try to clear my head and, and, you invited me up here."

"I think maybe you clear head too much!" again the laughter. "I know why you're in my cafe! Why are you here in China? I know your head is troubled... that so obvious!"

John studied his shoelaces, "Well, I'm here teaching in an international school, but, I don't really know if that's why I'm here. It's certainly not the main reason we came." He paused, "Wait, what do you mean it was so obvious my head is troubled?"

"How do you know a fish is a fish? I watch you walk down the street. You never look up. You shake your head like you are arguing with someone but no one there! Plain as day! Not exactly rocket surgery!"

LiuPing got up and crossed back over to the bar. "Ah yes, special tea is ready! No more time for question. You just wait one moment and we start to get you fixed back up."

Rather than the small delicate, almost effeminate, tea cups John was getting used to, LiuPing grabbed two large earthenware mugs and poured the strange concoction. "This peasant tea, strong stuff not meant for fragile little cups. Big cup warms cold, hard working, hands. Very good! Warms whole body. Very healthy!"

As he crossed over to where John was perched on the edge of his chair he held up one mug to fend off the inevitable question. "I said no time for question. This sweet ginger tea. You will like it!"

John took the offered cup and sat looking at it dubiously. Ginger tea? Ginger tea! He had eaten ginger in innumerable dishes in his life and it was ok but, he was pretty sure you weren't supposed to drink it. Were you? He looked over to LiuPing who was watching him with a look of great anticipation. John started to open his mouth.

"I said this no time for question!" LiuPing laughed. "Try it, you will like it."

John held the giant mug in both hands and stared down at its contents. The warm mug felt fantastic in his frozen hands. "Well this strange fellow has been right so far," he thought. He sniffed the steam rising from the translucent yellowish liquid. The aroma was intriguing. It was powerful but not at all unpleasant. It smelled a little like pepper but there was a sweetness there too. John had expected much worse. Throwing caution to the wind he raised the mug to his lips and sipped. The spicy sweet nectar seemed to wrap itself around his tongue and excite each taste bud individually. The enticing, exotic, almost indescribable flavor filled his entire mouth. He swallowed and felt incredible warmth flow down his throat and radiate through his chest. His eyes opened wide, "Wow!"

"I told you that you would like it!" LiuPing beamed. "Nothing better on a cold day."

As he took another sip John had to agree. This stuff was fantastic. He sank lower into the overstuffed chair and felt, well, he felt warm, warm inside and out. Even his mind felt more at ease, almost relaxed. He closed his eyes and with a long sigh he let out a breath that he felt he had been holding forever. He slowly opened his eyes to see LiuPing watching him with a satisfied smile.

"See, we're starting to get you fixed up! We take baby steps. Take long time."

John just stared at him. "What are you talking about?"

"Oh! Still no time for questions! Still too troubled!" LiuPing paused looking thoughtful, his smile gone for the moment. "You are teacher. Teachers often have troubled mind," he paused again.

John sipped his tea, content for the moment to simply sit in this warm place and see what this intuitive fellow has to say.

"Teacher who has left his home to teach far away must be very dedicated. Yet, you are troubled and say you don't know if teaching is why you are here. Very interesting. Maybe you are in the wrong place or, maybe you have the wrong vision. Which is it I wonder?" LiuPing got up and paced over to gaze out a window. He stood staring across the rooftop for so long John wondered if he had been forgotten.

"Hmmm. God doesn't bring people half-way round the world for no reason," LiuPing said softly coming back to the chair next to John. Astonished John wondered if LiuPing were actually a believer or if it was just a phrase he had picked up somewhere.

"I think maybe your story isn't finished yet. Yes, that's it! You have a story to tell which isn't finished yet. That's why your head is troubled and you are wandering."

"What are you talking about?" John blurted. "I'm not a storyteller, I'm just a teacher and I'm not even sure I'm suposed to be that."

"Oh yes! You have a story to tell but you don't know what it is yet. You just need to find it! That's even better!" LiuPing smiled like he had just won the lottery.

John just sat there shaking his head. "Yes, I'm troubled," he began slowly. "Before coming here things were so clear. We knew what we were doing, what we were called to do, and God did impossible things to bring us here. It was so exciting. Now, I just don't know," he paused, sipped his tea again feeling the warmth course through him. "Teaching anywhere is hard but, here it is so messed up, so confused. What they are doing, making me do, is so backwards from anywhere I've ever taught. I knew teaching in a Christian school would be different but come on, some of this is ridiculous! I'm trying to figure it out, how to make all the crazy pieces of what the school is doing here fit together so that it will actually work but I just can't. I've tried. It takes all of my time and isn't even why I came here. I wanted to come to help people, orphans, but, I don't even have time to spend with my own kids. I don't even have time to tell them a bedtime story! I don't know why God brought me here. I'm not doing any good for anyone," he paused for breath. "How on earth can you think I have a story to tell?"

"Aiya, I think now maybe you are too warmed up. Sit back and enjoy your tea. Relax a bit. From the beginning teachers have been searching for the right way. Very difficult." LiuPing paused looking thoughtful again. "So much to fix with this one Lord," he said under his breath looking up. John, still worked up but doing his best to calm down and drink his tea, didn't notice.

"Do you know where all the trouble began with this teaching thing?"

John laughed, "The beginning of time?"

"Ah good, you can still laugh, make joke. That's very good," LiuPing smiled. "There is hope for you yet John. Let me get you more tea and I'll tell you a story. Maybe it will help. Yes, I think it may help!"

"I don't see how a story is going to help me. I really should get home." John looked like he was going to get up but LiuPing was already across the room and before John knew it he had another full steaming mug of ginger tea in his hands. Not wanting to be rude he decided to make the best of it and settled back into the warm embrace of the chair.

THREE

"This story very very old, more than three thousand years," LiuPing began. "There was a great inventor, very famous. He invented many great and useful things, things that helped all people. All the people loved him and he grew very wealthy and wise. His name was FuXia but, no one called him by his name, everyone call him 'The Master'!

FuXia grew old and no longer invented things himself. Instead he trained a very clever apprentice whose name was Ts'ang Chieh. Now, Ts'ang Chieh was a very clever inventor indeed, almost as clever as The Master himself, but he was not so old and not so very wise. Sometimes he invented things that were not useful and sometimes he invented things that could cause great harm. The Master had always exercised great caution with his own inventions. He knew there were things that could be made which might look like wonderful things but which could actually cause great harm. The Master knew that in time Ts'ang Chieh would grow in wisdom and would himself be able to judge if something were good or bad. However, for the time being, he wanted to keep an eye on what Ts'ang Chieh was creating. So, every other month on the new moon Ts'ang Chieh brought all he had been working on and presented it to The Master to be evaluated.

Now, it was the day before the new moon and Ts'ang Chieh had been working very hard. With all his heart he wanted to please The Master with his inventions. This time he had created some wonderful things and he was sure The Master would give him great praise.

He had been working so very hard and it was a warm day so he decided to take a walk along the river in the cool shade of the great trees that grew there. As he walked along he noticed tracks of some type of an animal in the damp mud of the riverbank. Being of a curious nature he stopped to examine them more closely to see if he could figure out what had made the meandering tracks. Try as he might he could not. Frustrated but not yet defeated, he decided to sit in a hollow under a great tree and wait, hoping that whatever creature had made the tracks would return and he would have his answer. He waited and waited but there was nothing. After a while all his hard work caught up with him and he dozed off.

He awoke to the sound of footsteps, stealthy footsteps. He was very startled and as he struggled to clear the cobwebs of sleep from his brain and gain his feet he heard something very fast dash off along the riverbank headed upstream. Ts'ang Chieh saw it was now late in the day and would be getting dark soon. He needed to get home. It wasn't safe to be out after dark... one might get eaten. Those thoughts and the realization that some creature had gotten very close to him as he slept frightened him and he burst out from under the tree in a dash. He didn't make it more than three steps before he tripped over something, something covered in coarse fur, smelling like death itself, crouching in the path.

Ts'ang Chieh lie face down in the dust of the path whimpering softly, waiting for the pain of wild fangs tearing into his flesh he knew was imminent. Realizing his life was about to end, disappointment coursed though him, 'I haven't even invented anything important yet!' This one thought fired his courage and he resolved that he would not be an easy meal for a beast. He was meant for greater things than that.

Summoning all his strength, with a primal scream Ts'ang Chieh sprang to his feet and whirled to face his fate. He was prepared to fight to the death with his bare hands and teeth. He was prepared to face the fear and pain the next moments, possibly the last of his life, would bring. He was prepared to fight for his life against a great and wild beast and, maybe, lose. He was not prepared for the laughter that erupted from the beast or the ridicule.

'You silly little man. You scare away the fine stag I've been tracking without even a glimpse of it since morning but planned on eating for dinner. You run over me as I'm minding my own business trying to recover its trail. And, now you want to fight?' The fur clad figure laughed, 'You're so scrawny I wouldn't even break a sweat fighting you. And the way you scream!' At this the figure burst into such a laughing fit he finally had to sit down in the dusty path and put his head between his knees in order to catch his breath.

For his own part Ts'ang Chieh just stood there, mouth agape, staring at the convulsing hunter. 'Yes, he must be a hunter,' Ts'ang Chieh thought, 'no one else would dress so ridiculously or, smell so bad.' He scrunched-up his nose and, trying to regain some dignity said, 'I'm sorry. I was asleep under the tree and something startled me. Then, I tripped over you in the path and thought you were some kind of beast and that I was sure to be eaten alive. Naturally I felt I needed to defend myself.'

'Defend yourself! Defend yourself? Is that what you were doing?' Again the hunter launched into another uncontrolled fit of laughter.

At first Ts'ang Chieh was offended but, as he thought more about it he realized just how ridiculous he must look to someone who survived by killing wild animals. Surely he would be no match for the hunter, or, especially for the beast he had imagined was stalking him. He started to laugh along with the hunter. Suddenly something occurred to Ts'ang Chieh, something the hunter had said.

'Wait, wait. You said that you were tracking a great stag but, you haven't even seen it! How do you know it was a stag, let alone a great one?

'Well, by its tracks of course. You can learn many things about an animal by its tracks,' the hunter replied.

Ts'ang Chieh thought back to his frustration with the tracks in the mud earlier in the day. Maybe this hunter could help. 'I saw some interesting tracks earlier and was trying to figure out what had made them but, I couldn't. That's why I fell asleep under the tree... I was waiting for whatever made the tracks to return. Do you think maybe you could look at the tracks and tell me what made them?' The hunter simply nodded his head and Ts'ang Chieh led him over to where he had seen the curious tracks.

The hunter knelt down and studied the tracks. He lightly pressed on the mud along the edges. He picked up a small piece of mud and rolled it into a ball between his fingers. He sniffed it. With an air of solemn finality he said, 'Waiting for these animals to return won't work. They are very rare and only pass through this place once a lifetime. It is very rare indeed to even see their tracks for you see; these are the tracks of the Fenghuang."

Ts'ang Chieh gasped, 'The Fenghuang, the phoenix bird!? That's impossible they are things of legend! It's said they no longer walk the Earth. How can you know that these are the tracks of the king of all birds?'

The hunter shrugged, 'It's really quite simple. I was taught to hunt and track by my grandfather, who was taught by his grandfather, who was in turn taught by his grandfather, as is the way of our people. In this way none of the old things are forgotten. My grandfather taught me to see through the tracks to the animal beyond them. You see, each and every animal's track is different and these differences point to the differences in the animals themselves. In this way, the tracks of an individual animal will also change as the animal changes. One who has been taught to see these things, as my grandfather taught me, can look at the tracks and see the animal. Now, I have never in my life looked upon the tracks of the Fenghuang but, my great-great grandfather did and he has passed that knowledge to the generations who followed him. I know that these are the tracks of the king of birds,' he paused. 'This is a day of great joy as all have believed that the Fenghuang no longer walks the earth. But, it is also a day of sadness as I can see from the tracks that this bird is very old and has little life remaining. I believe it may be the last of its kind. These tracks are a powerful omen of great change in the world.'

At this the hunter stopped talking. He ignored the rapid-fire questions Ts'ang Chieh shot at him. A faraway look came into his eyes and he walked off following the almost forgotten trail of the stag.

Ts'ang Chieh started back toward home his mind filled with wonder. Imagine, he had found tracks of the great Fenghuang! This was indeed a wonderful find but what did it mean? Things like this were believed to be omens of things to come. 'I must be on the verge of a great invention,' Ts'ang Chieh thought. 'But, what could it possibly be? Certainly none of the inventions I have for The Master tomorrow.'

Sleep came very hard for Ts'ang Chieh that night. When he awoke it was early morning. He had slept restlessly and his dreams were filled with great birds and the words of the hunter filled his head '...can see through the tracks and see the animal beyond them.' Something about that phrase haunted him. He needed more time to think before he saw The Master.

He called for his servant Paopao. Ts'ang Chieh rarely trusted Paopao as he tended to be a bit mischievous. Paopao also wanted to be an inventor but his creativity only extended to stretching the truth and making excuses and he was not above saying the ideas of others belonged to him. Still, the boy had some uses if he were supervised. No matter, the errand for today required no creativity.

'Paopao, you are to go to The Master's compound and give him a message.' Paopao looked disappointed.

'Now pay attention! You are to tell The Master that I am working on a great invention but, it is not ready yet. Regretfully, I will not be able to come today but will have something wonderful to show him in two moons time.'

'But, what are you working on that's so important that you won't go see The Master?' Paopao began. 'He might be angry... angry at me, the simple messenger,' he whined.

'You should not be so worried about The Master being angry with you when I'm much closer to you boy!'

'But, what are you working on? I haven't seen you start anything new.'

'You miserable wretch! How dare you question me! Now, deliver my message immediately or it will be back to the pig farm for you!'

As Paopao scurried off, Ts'ang Chieh began to pace. '...can look through the tracks and see the animal... why does that seem so important?'

He decided it might help to go back to the riverbank and study the tracks again. He turned and hurried off to the place he had seen the tracks of the great Fenghuang the day before without even taking the time to eat breakfast. To his great dismay the tracks were no longer there. A great sadness washed over him and he slumped to the ground right on the river's edge, the wet of the early morning dew soaking through his clothing. A wave of despair washed over him as he realized he had not only not gone to meet The Master but he had also promised a great invention in two moons time. What a fool he was. He had nothing, not even the tracks remained. Maybe it was all a dream. Maybe he himself should go work the pig farm.

As he sat in the cold wet grass thinking even colder thoughts, the sun rose in the sky and, oblivious to Ts'ang Chieh's plight, the day warmed. Still Ts'ang Chieh sat unmoving. So still he sat, a wild cormorant, taking a break from chasing fish, swam up to the muddy bank where he was sitting, waddled up and sat right at Ts'ang Chieh's feet. Ts'ang Chieh stared at the prints the ungainly bird had made in the mud, so different than those of the mighty Fenghuang. '...can look through the tracks and see the animal.'

He began to think, 'How can you see the animal?'

A large fish sucked an insect from the still surface of the river creating radiating concentric rings. 'Nice fish,' he immediately thought, 'but, how do I know that? How do I know a fish is indeed a fish?'

He looked again at the tracks in the mud. 'So different from the tracks of the Fenghuang, and,' he paused, 'so very different from the tracks of the fish.'

Suddenly it hit him and he shouted startling the cormorant. 'The tracks, those scratches in the mud, represent what made them.' He stopped, smiled. 'Everything in the world has different tracks... what if everything could be represented by scratches in the mud!"

The ringing of John's cell phone yanked him back into the twenty-first century. It was his wife wondering where he was. It was getting dark and he was late and she was worried and the kids needed a bath. John hung up, sighed, his respite over.

"I've got to go," he said. "I really appreciate you trying to help me. The tea was great but, I'm afraid I don't understand the story at all."

LiuPing laughed, "Of course you don't understand story! It's just starting!"

"Well, I'm sorry I won't get to hear the rest of it." John stood and started for his jacket. "I really need to go but, could you explain one thing real fast? What was all that about 'scratches in the mud'?"

"You really don't understand! So much to learn before your story is ready! Oh well, we take baby steps. Just like eating an elephant!"

John just stood there looking confused. He shook his head and started to tie his scarf. "Eating an elephant?"

"One bite at a time!" LiuPing chuckled. "You come back soon. I tell you more of the story!"

John headed for the door. As he headed down the stairwell LiuPing called down to him, "Hey California, you want the answer to the scratches in the mud?"

John answered back, only a little sarcastically, "I'd love some answers!"

"The scratches in the mud... Ts'ang Chieh invented writing!"

John's last thoughts as he headed home were, "Well, that explains a lot around here."

FOUR

Two weeks passed before John knew it. Weeks filled with teaching and meetings and grading and more meetings. Questions and doubts still tormented him. He had little time to think, well, to think real thoughts anyway, but that was something of a mixed blessing. Every so often, while sitting in a meeting about standards or assessment or "Biblical Integration" (whatever that is) his mind would wonder, just for a moment, to a warm cozy place filled with green where a slightly deranged storyteller told a meaningless tale. He would chuckle inwardly to himself, "scratches in the mud!"

He had no intention of seeing how that story ended. After all, why would he want to hear about some ancient success story? And, all that nonsense about he himself having a story to tell. What rubbish! How on earth was that going to help him today? He had much bigger things to worry about like rewriting the school's English standards, and "Vertical Articulation", and some nonsensical school-wide learning results that were impossible to quantify, oh, and "Biblical Integration"... can't forget about that. He didn't have time for stories no matter how pleasant the atmosphere.

Finally a two-week holiday came. John, again hoping to clear his head, set out on another walk hoping it wouldn't become quite the adventure the last one had. This time upon crossing the street, wanting to be sure to avoid a certain LiuPing Cafe and its loquacious proprietor, he turned right.

The day was even colder than the last time he had ventured out but, at least heading in this direction, the wind was at his back making it much more tolerable. He walked on, intently focused on where he was stepping, putting one foot in front of the other without extraneous thought. Just walk.

He had traveled some distance this way without so much as a glance at the city around him when suddenly a strong gust of wind blew the hood of his parka off his head leaving his closely cropped scalp to be ravaged by the cold. He stopped momentarily confused. "That gust came from the front!" he thought aloud. "How did the wind change direction so quickly?" As he stood there, head uncovered, freezing and trying to make sense of what had happened he heard a high, excited voice.

"Hey California! You come back!"

John looked up only to see the foreboding stairwell and the sign "LiuPing Cafe."

"I'm so happy you come back!" LiuPing was beaming. "Ready for another bite of the elephant?"

John stared, stammered, "How did I get here?"

"You walked you crazy man. Aiya, still have no sense, you going to freeze! You should take taxi to come visit when it this cold! You should have called before coming. Cafe is closed. It's important holiday! Close for two weeks!"

"But, I walked the other way! Why am I here?"

"Ah, still full of questions I see. Why are you here? Why are any of us here? Very old question! Better question than you had last time. Making progress! Well come on up, we work on fixing you up."

At this LiuPing started up the stairs. John, still too confused to argue, followed and soon found himself settled into the now familiar chair with a steaming mug in his hands, warmth washing over him. He closed his eyes, smiled. This really wasn't so bad.

When John opened his eyes he saw LiuPing, who had again taken the seat next to him, sitting with his hands folded in his lap, looking at the ceiling, muttering something John couldn't quite make out. When he noticed John looking at him, he broke into his characteristic smile, leaned forward, put his elbows on his knees and his chin on his still folded hands.

"Today I make one rule. I see you still have troubled head so; I let you ask one question. If it is a good one maybe you will get an answer. I don't think you're ready to start asking right questions yet!"

"Ok. But, I really didn't come here to ask questions anyway..." John began.

"Maybe not, maybe not, but I see you coming down the street again... arguing with nobody. You are definitely full of questions. Very good thing!"

"It's a good thing I'm full of questions?"

"Aiya, I told you, only one question. You going to waste it on that?"

John chuckled and shook his head, "No, I guess not."

"That too bad! Pretty good question! Very good answer!" LiuPing smiled mischievously. "I give you a free answer... but this the only one! It's a good thing to be full of questions because only people who ask question get answer. People who are full of questions eventually ask big questions... very important questions. Very important answers. Help all mankind!"

"So, I have a story to tell about asking big questions!" John laughed. "That makes things so much easier! You know, there was a day I might have actually believed you. A day when I had the answers, the right answers. A day when I was the king of my realm. Now, I literally have no idea what I'm doing here. Seriously. I walked the opposite direction on the street I knew led to your cafe. I didn't want to come here and listen to another story... especially not about someone who makes a huge discovery and lives happily ever after," John paused. "Look, I really appreciate your hospitality and I love this place but, I don't think listening to ancient fairy tales is going to help solve the real problems I'm dealing with."

LiuPing smiled and looked to the ceiling. His lips moved slightly but no sound came out. After a moment and with a look of utter peace, he turned and fixed his eyes on John.

"I don't know all of the problems you are dealing with. Maybe they are not all so big? Sometimes hard to tell which problems are there to be fixed and which ones are there to fix you. Maybe you tell me the biggest problem that keeps your head so troubled? Maybe talking show us where to look for answers!"

John sighed, "Only one? I'm not even sure where to start. So many of the problems are related. Before I came here I really felt I knew how to teach. I was even named "Teacher of the Year" my first year back into teaching. Here things are very different. They are trying to use the same broken system used in public schools in the states here but they are trying to build it themselves and add two new layers on to it... layers that I can't see any way of reconciling. I'm trying to find a way to blend together a system that relies on measurable benchmarks and objectives with a system that is hoping for spiritual growth... How do you measure that? The philosophies just don't match."

"That is a indeed a big problem. It's no wonder you go walking out in the cold. But... this isn't a new problem. Actually very, very old!"

"Why do I get the idea you've got another story to tell?" John groaned.

LiuPing exclaimed, "Aiya California, you very wrong!" He smiled a mischievous grin, "It's the same story! We've only just started it!"

"You're kidding right? How is a story about that Ts'ang Chieh guy getting famous thousands of years ago and living happily ever after going to help?"

"Aiya, so many questions! I'm just going to ignore questions until you ask a good one. I told you this will be like eating an elephant. Take long time! Have to stop and digest many times. Besides, story doesn't end the way you think it does! Now, drink your tea and no more questions. You may find this big problem has easy answer!"

FIVE

"Now where did we leave off? Oh yes, Ts'ang Chieh was sitting on the river bank wondering if maybe, just maybe, everything in the world could be expressed by scratches in the mud and if so, what would that mean. He sat there thinking and scribbling in the mud with a stick until late in the afternoon when Paopao, concerned he might be missing some great thing to copy, found him there.

'Master Ts'ang Chieh! You have been gone all day and I was worried about you. I have a message for you from The Master.'

Ts'ang Chieh looked up from his scribbles with a look of triumph. 'I have been here all day working on something amazing! I think it will change the entire world.'

Paopao looked around for the wonderful invention but all he could see was Ts'ang Chieh sitting in the mud scribbling with a stick. His poor master must have gone insane from the constant pressure of having to invent things himself he thought. He made a vow to himself never to let it happen to him. It was so much easier to steal other people's ideas.

'But master, where is this great thing you speak of? I see nothing but strange scratches in the mud.'

'Aiya, my blind apprentice. You truly do not see! Those scratches in the mud are the great thing. They contain the whole world! But, you are too simple of mind to be able to see it. Maybe you are better suited to the pig farm after all.'

'Surely you are correct master,' inwardly Paopao was seething. 'But, you have been sitting in the hot sun all day. Maybe the sun has hurt your eyes. You should rest and take some refreshment.'

'There is nothing wrong with my eyes you foolish servant! But, you are correct. It has been a long hot day and I should take better care of myself. Ts'ang Chieh pried himself up off the muddy bank and turned to the path toward home. 'Wait, you said you have a message for me from The Master?'

'Yes, yes. The Master was not pleased that you did not come today... that you didn't even care to come yourself to explain but sent me, your humble servant.' Paopao saw an opportunity to get a little revenge. 'I tried to explain to him that you were working on something very important but, since I'm only fit to be a pig farmer and not the great Ts'ang Chieh's worthy apprentice, when he questioned me I got nervous. I may have accidentally told him you thought your project was even more important than him.'

'You did what! You worthless dog! How dare you say such lies to the master! Surely I will send you back to the farm!' Ts'ang Chieh was seething with anger. 'How did The Master respond? Tell me quickly or you will sleep with the pigs this very night!'

Paopao, knowing he had pushed too far and that if he were sent away he'd never be able to become a wealthy, powerful inventor, instantly threw himself in the dirt at Ts'ang Chieh's feet.

'Aiya! Master please forgive your worthless servant! No harm came from my mistake for The Master was not angry, just disappointed. He said he was sad that you could not come today because he values the time you spend together!'

'You worthless creature! You swear you speak the truth now? How am I to ever trust you?'

'Yes master, I swear this is true. The Master was sad that you could not spend time together, but he said he understood. He said this was the mark of a great inventor... to put all else aside and follow inspiration when it hits. He praised you in front of all his advisers and said that when he was young he would often do the same thing. He ordered me, your worthless servant, to tell you that he hopes you could join him before two moons pass... hopefully on the next moon. But, he also said to follow your inspiration. He is excited to see where it will lead. Please don't send me away.' Paopao finished in a flurry placing his forehead on Ts'ang Chieh's feet.

'If you are telling the truth this is good news and I will let you stay, unless you disappoint me again. You will receive no more chances from me.' Ts'ang Chieh started up the path home. 'Yes, this is a very good thing indeed. I will work every day and be able to share this wonderful new thing I have created with The Master on the next moon. It will be a day to remember.'

So the next morning, and each of the twenty six that followed it, Ts'ang Chieh woke early and went down to the river bank. Of all the mornings, the first was the hardest. When Ts'ang Chieh had arrived at the familiar bank he was mortified to find that in the night, of all the muddy banks along the placid river, a water buffalo had chosen his to wallow in, erasing all of his work from the day before. At first he had slumped to his knees in despair but Ts'ang Chieh quickly realized this work was too important to be undone by something as simple as a water buffalo. He also realized that keeping this wonderful invention on the riverbank was foolish. It wouldn't do any good for anyone sitting there in the mud. It needed to be portable. He quickly decided that this could finally be a chance for his worthless servant to earn his keep. Ts'ang Chieh designed a shallow wooden box about as wide and as tall as a man's hand and as thick as his thumb. Every day Paopao spent endless hours building these boxes, filling them full to the top with mud and smoothing the surface before carrying them to where Ts'ang Chieh sat under the great tree and scratched strange designs onto them. Paopao would then lay the boxes in the sun to dry.

To his credit, Paopao worked hard but he truly thought his master's mind had cracked. What kind of invention was boxes of dried mud with scribbles on it? He himself had better ideas than that! He should just go back to the farm on his own... he wouldn't have to work so hard there. He was baffled that Ts'ang Chieh seemed to get more and more excited with each new box. These worthless little boxes couldn't even be used as bricks. They were far too fragile as he found when he dropped one and it shattered. Master was not happy then! Paopao was pretty sure this was all going to end badly when The Master came to see what Ts'ang Chieh had been working on and found it was nothing but mud pies. He wanted to be there to see him disgraced so, he worked on.

Day after day they toiled on until, almost before they knew it, it was the day before the new moon. They had completed more than one hundred boxes. Paopao had never seen Ts'ang Chieh so excited as they carefully wrapped each box with red fabric, loaded them onto a cart, and covered it with a blanket. So happy was Ts'ang Chieh as they pushed the cart home that he even praised Paopao.

'You have done great work these last days Paopao. You have made me proud and I am sorry that I called you worthless in the past. I truly would not have been able to complete this great work without your help. I want you to be with me tomorrow when I share this gift for all mankind with The Master. I will also need your help to place the boxes in the correct order. It will be a glorious day!'

Paopao, still convinced Ts'ang Chieh was insane, replied with a chuckle, 'I wouldn't miss it for the world!'

The next day dawned bright and clear. There was just a touch of chill in the air pointing to a long awaited end to the blistering heat of summer. Harvest time with its bountiful riches and grand festivals was just around the corner. Ts'ang Chieh couldn't help but think just how wonderful this time would be this year. Surely, thanks to his wonderful new invention, he would be seated alongside The Master at the head table with all the village elders. His time had come at last.

Ts'ang Chieh wasn't to meet with The Master until after the mid-day meal yet he and Paopao left for The Master's compound right after breakfast. They had much work to do and everything had to be perfect. As Ts'ang Chieh and Paopao slowly pushed the loaded cart through the village streets people shouted questions at them. Everyone had heard that this time Ts'ang Chieh had created something truly wonderful and they couldn't wait to discover what it was.

Soon a small crowd began to follow and Ts'ang Chieh began to get a little nervous. What if The Master didn't understand what he had created? What if the people weren't ready yet for this type of invention? What if they didn't understand and laughed at him? Paopao surely didn't understand. Why would the others in the village? He would be laughed at, again. He would fail. He didn't know if he could stand another failure but, what could he do? They were already at the gates which opened into The Masters courtyard. He needed to think of something quickly. 'Too late now,' he thought as the exuberant crowd whisked them through the gates, into the courtyard, and stopped at the very feet of The Master himself.

By now you've heard of The Master enough to probably have formed a pretty clear vision of what he looks like in your mind... a shrunken old man with blazing white hair and a stark white beard both of which reached nearly to his feet. He would be wearing flowing white robes and be stooped and gnarled and wrinkled and walk hunched over with a stick to help hold him up. This is after all what one thinks of when they hear someone called 'the master' and even more so when it is capitalized 'The Master' but, this vision you have is not The Master of this story. In fact, The Master was very old but his age was deceiving. He was thin and of average height and he stood ramrod straight. His face was indeed wrinkled but it was with the type of wrinkles that radiate from one's eyes and spoke more of much laughter and many smiles and maybe just a bit too much squinting off at unseen horizons than of old age. His head and face, except for a long thin drooping mustache that gyrated in the wind like the tail of a kite, were shaved clean and tanned the color of polished leather. Though he was even richer than he was old, he wore simple clothes more suited to the local blacksmith than to the most celebrated man of his time. He always had a short, sturdy, razor-sharp knife tucked into his belt because he said he never wanted to be caught without his most useful tool. What was most notable about him though were his eyes. His eyes never seemed to age. They were brilliant and piercing. They were the kind of eyes that seemed to be able to see directly into one's soul. The kind of eyes that in a glance would make a brave and righteous man proud and make those of lesser character cower. They spoke of great intelligence and wisdom but also of great kindness. His eyes always held a sparkle that made children laugh. Those were the eyes that looked upon Ts'ang Chieh as the cart rolled to a stop.

'Ts'ang Chieh! Welcome! It has been much too long since you have honored my home with your company!' The Master embraced Ts'ang Chieh warmly. 'I always enjoy our time together and seeing how you think. And I hear you have invented something wonderful, of great importance! Even more important than spending time with me last moon eh?' At this The Master winked and slapped Ts'ang Chieh on the back. 'I can't wait to see and hear all about this wonderful thing! I always knew you had greatness in you!'

Ts'ang Chieh smiled from ear to ear. How could one have such doubts when confronted with the enthusiasm of The Master? His fate lay in The Master's hands and he trusted The Master's judgment explicitly but, the common people could be fickle. Care must still be taken. It was the wise thing to do.

'Master, I apologize for my absence. I have indeed been focused on my labors as of late and have truly missed your company as well. I have been looking forward to sharing what I've been working on with you but, I'm afraid it's not totally complete and I, well, I ... I don't know that it is ready for the whole world to see it. I know that you will be able to see it and know it for what it is but the common people...'

'Ah my young friend, I see that you have grown in wisdom since we have last met! Often the world is either not ready for or not able to understand great new things. It takes wisdom indeed to show restraint at the very times it is hardest to, for well I know it is nearly impossible to restrain oneself after the heady rush of discovering something truly new. It's even harder when you think it's something big enough to change the world. Sometimes, as an inventor it's impossible as you can be too close to your work to truly see it for what it is. I am proud to see how much you have grown. I only wish that I had possessed such wisdom at your age.'

Ts'ang Chieh didn't know how to respond. He knew there was no way he could tell The Master the truth... that he wanted to share in private out of fear rather than out of wisdom. Thankfully, The Master continued.

'I know just the place for you to show me what you've created. It's completely away from prying eyes and ears and is one of my favorite spots. Come let me show you.'

Ts'ang Chieh turned, 'Paopao, stay here and don't let anyone near the cart... make sure you keep it covered! I'll be back soon.'

Ts'ang Chieh followed The Master into his house and then up several flights of stairs and finally up a tall ladder that was braced against one wall and poked through a hole in the lofty ceiling. By the time Ts'ang Chieh reached the top he was breathing heavily but The Master didn't seem even the least bit winded.

"Master, I mean no disrespect but, how is it that at your age you are not even breathing hard after that climb while I, a man in my prime can't catch my breath or still my heart?'

'Just because I'm old doesn't mean I've totally stopped inventing.' The Master said with a twinkle in his eyes. 'You should drink more hot water!'

'But Master, that's nothing new. We have been drinking hot water for generations to improve our health.'

The Master pulled a gnarled yellow piece of root from a leather pouch that hung from his belt.

'Ah, but next time you must try and boil it with a large piece of this yellow root and several pieces of the tall sweet cane that grows along the river. It will fix you right up!'

Ts'ang Chieh looked at the proffered root. It certainly didn't look like anything special and it didn't smell very pleasant. He wasn't sure he wanted to drink anything made from it but, The Master was wise in many things. He would indeed try it.

He took a moment to take in his surroundings. Ts'ang Chieh knew when they started up the ladder that they were going up on the roof but what he found there amazed him. The Master had transformed his otherwise normal rooftop into a veritable garden oasis. There were plants of every description. In the middle was a small pond teaming with colorful fish. Amazingly, a small stream meandered from what looked like an ordinary, though perpetually overflowing bucket sitting under a wooden framework that supported a strange spinning blade on the opposite end of the roof, and splashed over a small waterfall into the pond. Ts'ang Chieh stood mesmerized studying the pond. For all his cleverness he could not see how such a thing could exist up on the roof. How did the pond not overfill and flood the entire roof? How was a non-ending stream issuing from a small bucket? What was the purpose of the spinning blade? The entire thing made no sense at all.

After a few moments The Master gently took him by the arm and led him to a meticulously crafted but somehow still rustic wooden bench that sat near the stream and was shaded by three trees of a type Ts'ang Chieh had never seen before. They sat in silence for a moment lulled by the quiet gurgle of the stream. The view from where they sat was amazing.

'This is my private spot,' The Master began. 'No one is allowed up here, ever. It's where I come to think and to get perspective. From here it seems that I can almost see the whole of nature and humanity.'

'It's true,' Ts'ang Chieh thought. From up here you could look down on the village or your eyes could look over the farmland to where the lazy river cut its meandering course through the long valley. 'From here one could see what mattered.'

'So my young friend, do you think this is a private enough place to share your creation? There is a bare area on the other side of the roof that you could set up what you have brought today.'

'Yes Master, I think this is the perfect place. With your permission I will have Paopao start bringing up the pieces so you can see it after the noon meal as we had planned.'

'By all means! I will have one of my servants help him and you and I can sit here in the shade just a bit longer. I really have missed spending time with you."

SIX

"Time for more tea!" LiuPing paused and scurried over to the bar. "So, what do you think of my story so far? And remember... No questions!"

"Well, I still don't see how this is going to help me and I really don't understand how Ts'ang Chieh could possibly be nervous. I mean, he invented writing for Pete's sake. That's got to be one of the greatest achievements in history. How can that be bad? The man was a genius! I wonder why I've never heard of him?"

"Very interesting. It's so easy to see any technology that has been around longer than oneself as good. It's been there forever. It has to be good right? Not always the case!"

"Oh come on! We're talking about writing here... writing. Where would the world be without it?"

"Hey, I said no question... especially not questions that big with no possible answers! Where would the world be without writing? Silly question... impossible to answer! Maybe something to think about California, how many of your troubles right now are a result of Ts'ang Chieh?"

John got up and paced across the room, stared out of the window across the dormant garden to the hidden horizon beyond. LiuPing had a point he grudgingly accepted. But, blaming someone dead more than four thousand years wasn't going to do him much good. Interesting thought though, no matter how irrelevant to real life it was.

"Tea is ready! Come... sit... the story will continue!"

Still in thought, John wandered back to his chair and took the mug LiuPing offered him. He stared down into the depth of the cup as if looking for answers and saw... large pieces of yellow root drifting in circles at the bottom of the mug. He looked up in surprise. Before he could speak LiuPing laughed out.

"Of course! I told you last time this drink very old! You drink The Masters invention for long happy life... ginger tea!"

John simply shook his head.

"With the help of The Master's servant, Paopao was able to carry all one hundred of the carefully wrapped boxes to the roof in what seemed like no time at all. As The Master and his servant went downstairs to see about preparations for the mid-day meal, Ts'ang Chieh and Paopao set to the task of unwrapping and carefully arranging the boxes. Getting things set up took longer than Ts'ang Chieh thought it would because he had to continually reset the order of the boxes. For his part Paopao could not understand why Ts'ang Chieh kept getting so angry with him.

'Master, why does it matter so much which order the boxes are in and which end is up? I don't understand why this one goes this way and that one goes that way and why this one is so important that it simply must be first in line. They are just lines scratched in mud. Does it really matter?'

'Ah my servant, I know you have been working long and hard. You are tired and you do not see the great design behind all of this. Be assured that what we are doing right now is of the utmost importance. If the boxes are not placed just so it all becomes meaningless.'

'But master, it appears meaningless to me no matter which order the boxes are in!'

'Be patient just a while longer young one. I promised you that you would be with me when I present this great thing to The Master and soon, you alone shall be. Then you will understand the importance of all our labor these past days. It will be a time of rejoicing!'

'And of laughter too I think!' Paopao replied with a grin.

'Yes, a time of laughter and rejoicing for all people!' Ts'ang Chieh was truly starting to feel better, his earlier misgivings completely forgotten.

As they were just finishing arranging the last boxes, The Master's servant called them to come and eat. There were two kinds of meals at The Master's home... rich and extravagant or simple and homey reminiscent of The Master's peasant roots. Ts'ang Chieh was so excited and nervous that if asked later, he would not have been able to tell you which type of meal it was. Paopao, on the other hand, could have told you in great detail just how disappointed he was with the plain bland food he was served, surely someone as rich and powerful as The Master deserved to eat better and certainly should treat his guests better. He decided that when he was famous every meal would be a celebration.

In time everyone ate their fill and it was time, finally time, for Ts'ang Chieh to share his fantastic discovery with The Master. With great, though very different expectations, the trio headed up the ladder to the rooftop, Paopao lagging slightly behind. As they approached the curious collection of mud filled wooden boxes Paopao stayed a respectable distance behind the elder inventors. He hoped to appear subservient but, truth be told, even though he was anxious indeed to see master Ts'ang Chieh humbled, he didn't actually want be too closely associated with the failure he expected to see. He still planned on having a successful career someday! They stood looking at the boxes for some time in silence; The Master was the first to speak.

'Well Ts'ang Chieh, you certainly have been busy. This is an impressive amount of work.' He bent to look at one of the boxes more closely. 'And, the craftsmanship you have exhibited in these boxes is very fine, very fine indeed!'

Ts'ang Chieh was beaming. Paopao was laughing so hard inside he was afraid he would not be able to contain himself. His mirth was short lived however as he found himself pulled into much greater association with this mess than he ever wanted.

'Thank you Master, it has been much work indeed. I can't take credit for the craftsmanship of the boxes however. It was my design but, my young apprentice Paopao here did all of the work. In fact he is responsible for most of what you see here.'

Paopao had a moment of panic and blurted, 'No Master that is not true! I did a little bit of work, but only what Master Ts'ang Chieh told me to do. To tell the truth, I don't even know why I had to make all of these boxes or what their purpose is... if there even is one.' The last line was said under his breath. He wasn't quite as stupid as some people made him out to be.

The Master turned to look at Paopao more closely. He squinted slightly as if smelling something unpleasant and then turned his attention back to the boxes.

'Well my worthy apprentice, it seems that your servant doesn't think too highly of what you have brought me today. In truth, if I were far more foolish than I am, and I didn't know you so well, I might seriously question this invention of yours. After all, it looks like all you did was make some dainty little boxes, filled them with mud, and made a few strange scratches on them with a stick.'

Ts'ang Chieh opened his mouth to respond but The Master cut him off before he could start.

'No, let me continue! I have known you a long time Ts'ang Chieh and you have never disappointed me, never wasted my time with something frivolous. So, I must believe there is something to these boxes of dried mud, something that is not so easy to see at first glance. Something beyond what the simpleton sees... After all, Paopao has spent many hours working on this with you and he truly does not see. Interesting, let me study this for a moment and see if I have more insight than your young servant.'

The Master retreated to the shade of a small citrus tree, close enough to be able to see all of the boxes clearly, and sat cross-legged with his elbows on his knees and his chin on his right fist. From time to time he would look up at Ts'ang Chieh and comment.

'It's not the boxes themselves ... They are exquisitely made but, really there isn't anything all that special about them.'

'It certainly can't be the mud, that's as common as ever.'

'Mud in a box is a novel idea but, there is no purpose to it, so, it must have something to do with the scribbles. Aiya.'

'There is something about the scribbles in the mud. I can't quite figure it out but, it seems as if they are all familiar somehow. Like I've seen them before but, I'm certain I haven't. Most interesting! Ts'ang Chieh, enlighten me. Am I at least on the right path? What is the secret of these scratches in the mud for I know these are what you have brought to me today... not the boxes of mud, but the scratches. Tell me, what do they mean?'

Ts'ang Chieh was beaming... The Master was on the right track and Ts'ang Chieh knew it would be very easy to explain everything to him.

'Yes Master, what I have brought you today is indeed the scratches in the mud. I call them characters. They each hold great meaning for you see; each of them is like a footprint of something in the mud. If you know just how to see them they point to the specific thing that made them. That's why they all seem familiar to you... I have captured in the characters the essence of something else. These boxes are just the start as I see that one could represent everything in the world in this manner either by one character or by combining several together.'

'Well, that is certainly interesting Ts'ang Chieh but, to what purpose? Couldn't someone just as well paint a picture of things? People have been painting things for years. If someone paints a fish, I can look and see it's a fish.'

'Master, with these characters one can tell a story. Let me show you.' Ts'ang Chieh moved a few tiles around. 'There, these characters now ask a question... "How do you know a fish is a fish?" Or, you can move these out of the way and add these here and here and now the characters give helpful information. "It is easiest to catch fish in the morning." So you see, you can combine the characters to almost any combination.'

'Hmmm, yes now I do see what you are saying. This is truly a new thing under the sun. Inventing this is an amazing accomplishment

Ts'ang Chieh! And yet, I wonder. We must always ask... Is this a good thing?'

'But Master don't you see, with characters one could record all the knowledge and wisdom of the ages! With them people will be able to remember everything and they will have great knowledge and wisdom! Isn't that a good thing? Isn't it a wonderful thing? So much knowledge would be available to everyone it would be the start of a golden age for our people!'

For what seemed like an eternity The Master sat frozen in silence. Then, he slowly rose to his feet and started to walk away from the wooden boxes with their characters etched in mud.

'Ts'ang Chieh come sit with me in my favorite spot where we can be away from the prying ears of your servant and we can look across the horizons and see what all this looks like from a different perspective.'

As The Master and Ts'ang Chieh headed across the roof Paopao flopped himself down in the shade and studied what he now knew were to be called characters. He frowned. Maybe master Ts'ang Chieh wasn't so crazy after all. He studied the characters and soon he was able to imagine that he could see the meaning behind each one. He suddenly realized the greatness of the idea. He burned with jealousy as he just knew that this would make Ts'ang Chieh one of the most famous men of all time... he would be even greater than The Master! What bothered him the most was that he saw no way to take this incredible new thing, possibly the greatest thing to be invented in his lifetime, and make it his own. He sat hugging his knees to his chest brooding, waiting for The Master to finish praising Ts'ang Chieh before telling everyone of his greatness.

Paopao would have been very surprised to hear the conversation that was taking place on the opposite end of the roof.

The Master was speaking.

'Ts'ang Chieh, don't be so upset. I truly think that what you have created could be one of the greatest things of all time. What I'm saying is; you, as the inventor, are too closely attached to your invention to be able to be the best judge of how or if it should be used. Inventors naturally see their inventions as wonderful helpful things but, they can rarely see the repercussions that might happen for even the greatest, most incredibly good things change other things simply by their use. This is not always bad as change is inevitable but, it is something that needs to be evaluated. With great ideas comes great responsibility!'

'But Master, how can this be a bad thing? Characters can be used to spread knowledge and wisdom. They can help the people to remember the things that are important! How can that be bad?'

'I think that if you open your mind and look closely you will see. You say characters can spread knowledge and wisdom. I wonder if that is true. I'm afraid that if people can simply look at characters to gain knowledge it could be very hard to know if they truly know something. For example, look across the valley there to where the potter has his workshop. What if you wanted a special pot made, one that is very important and must be perfect? How do you know if the potter can make that pot?'

'That's easy Master, you go and ask the potter. It will be obvious by how he answers if he knows how to make the pot.'

'That is true. But, what if the potter only knows how to answer because it is something they have seen in your characters? How will one be able to determine if someone really knows something if everyone has the right answers? And wisdom? That's even worse. Wisdom only comes through experience and someone who claims to be wise but is not can be very dangerous! How will we be able to know the wise from the foolish if the secrets of wisdom are shown to all with your characters?'

'But, what about memory? Surely you can't argue against characters helping to remember and preserve stories?'

'I'm afraid I can. I fear that if people can simply put the stories down in characters, to be looked at whenever they want, they won't feel the need to remember at all... the characters will do the remembering for them. No my young apprentice, I don't think this will help people remember at all.'

Ts'ang Chieh hung his head defeated.

'What then shall I do Master?'

'Ts'ang Chieh, be proud for this is really an incredible accomplishment, one beyond even me. Take heart, I need to think about this more before I'm ready to say if it is a good thing or bad. For now, bundle your boxes back up and keep them secret. Come again to my home in three weeks time and we will discuss this further.'

'As you wish Master.'

'Oh, and remember, until we speak again you must tell no one!'

'Yes Master.'

As The Master sat staring off at unseen horizons, Ts'ang Chieh found Paopao sitting as before with his forehead on his knees.

'Paopao let us wrap up all of our boxes again and return them to our cart.'

Paopao looked up startled, 'But master why? I thought you said this would be a day for rejoicing. Yet, you look very tired. Is everything ok? Was The Master displeased with your amazing discovery?'

'Ah Paopao, I am sorry. I promised you a day of celebration unlike any before. That day has not yet come though I'm certain it will soon. The Master would like to think about all of the changes that could happen if everyone started using my characters. We are to come back in three weeks and until that time we must discuss the characters with no one! The Master is very wise. I'm sure it will all work out for the best. You are correct though, I am suddenly so very tired and we have much work to do yet before we rest today.'

Paopao felt a surge of hope; maybe, just maybe this was the big opportunity he had been waiting for. Mustn't let master Ts'ang Chieh suspect anything.

'Master, this day has been long for you. Why don't you sit and rest and I will see to loading the wagon. I have been resting while you spoke with The Master.'

'That is very kind of you Paopao! I believe I will take that offer. Thank you.'

So, as Paopao carefully wrapped each of the one hundred boxes and carefully loaded them on the cart, Ts'ang Chieh rested in the shade.

Paopao had the cart loaded in record time and they started the long walk home. The journey took much longer than normal as the inquisitive crowds of the morning were now even more so and the questions rained down non-stop. Ts'ang Chieh grew increasingly irritated by the questioning. The Master had told him to keep the characters a secret and he had every intention of obeying.

'Aiya, can't they stop with all the questions?' Ts'ang Chieh suddenly blurted. 'I can't stand it anymore!'

'Master, let me try to talk to the people. I will explain that you are very tired and can't answer their questions right now. Maybe I can convince them to leave you alone for a while.'

Paopao walked over to the largest group of followers and spoke to them in low tones Ts'ang Chieh couldn't quite hear. Whatever he said must have been good because at the end several of the men shook Paopao's hand and, with a fair bit of whispering, the crowd dispersed.

The remainder of the journey went smoothly though once or twice Paopao needed to stop and speak with small groups of curious bystanders. In each case the people shook Paopao's hand and left in peace. Finally they reached Ts'ang Chieh's home. He wanted to crawl into his bed and sleep for a week but first he would have to hide the characters somewhere safe from prying eyes. Paopao noticed his fatigue and hesitation.

'Master, you have had a long day and are exhausted. Why don't you go in to rest and I will be sure the characters are well taken care of. It is not good for you to be so tired!'

'Paopao, that is most kind of you. I'm afraid I may have misjudged you and I am sorry. Today you have proven yourself to be of great worth to me. If you could see to putting the characters somewhere where they will be safe it would be wonderful. You have been working so hard lately. I don't think I will have need for you until we need to return to The Master's in three weeks. Why don't you take some time to rest and enjoy yourself? You have certainly earned a rest.'

'Thank you Master Ts'ang Chieh. I could use some rest as well! I will put the characters in a safe and secret place and return when you send for me. Rest well master!'

Ts'ang Chieh was already inside and on his way straight to bed."

LiuPing paused and glanced up at the clock. He jumped up with a start.

"Aiya! I forgot I have important meeting! You must go now! Come back tomorrow.... more story tomorrow!"

John was out the door and halfway down the stairs before he even thought to argue. He certainly didn't want to come back tomorrow. As he reached the sidewalk he heard LiuPing call down from above.

"Hey California, I forgot to answer your question!"

"But, I never asked a good one..."

"Oh but you did! You ask 'Why am I here?' You came here because the street is a big circle! No matter which way you go it leads to LiuPing Cafe!! Come back tomorrow! Ten o'clock!"

John chuckled to himself, "At least I don't have to think about which way to walk," and started for home.

SEVEN

That night after helping put the children to bed, John stretched out on the couch and thought about what he had heard that day. He knew it wasn't an accident that he had wound up at the LiuPing Cafe and that meant it had to be for a reason but what? One thing that stood out to him was the need to have the proper perspective. He understood exactly why The Master had created his rooftop garden and realized with a start that his new friend LiuPing had done the same thing. He suddenly longed to have such a place for his very own. He surely needed a place to contemplate things from an objective perspective.

The dog scratching at the door pulled him back to the present and with a groan he resigned himself to another of the nightly adventure walks in the cold with the dog. He bundled up, let his wife know what he was doing, scooped-up the dog, and headed out the door. As he stood waiting for the elevator something was pulling at the back of his mind. Something important but just out of reach. It hit him as he turned and saw the set of stairs leading up. He lived in a top floor apartment. There was nothing above but the roof but, could he get out onto it? A short climb brought him to a padlocked door at the top of the stairs. Out of curiosity he gave a short tug on the lock and instantly the entire hasp fell to pieces, rusted away. He opened the door and stepped out onto the roof. The wind pulled at his hood and sent darts of cold air shooting through any gaps in his layers of clothes. He sucked in a deep breath between clenched teeth and pulled a loop of his scarf up over his nose. It was bitterly cold but not unbearable and he laughed to himself that he must actually be getting used to the cold as unlikely as that might seem.

On first glance it seemed the only thing his rooftop had in common with The Master's was that it was on the top of a building. Instead of a lush garden the flat bare concrete roof contained a tangle of exposed pipes and wires and a small forest of satellite dishes and solar water heaters. It was all surrounded by a waist-high concrete wall. At first John was disappointed but as he put the squirming dog down the place began to grow on him. For starters, there didn't seem to be anything of danger for the dog or anything that would allow it to get into mischief. It was unusual to be able to let the dog roam on its own and John found it very freeing. The dog could get his exercise and do his nightly business and John could get some quality quiet time. He walked over to the edge of the roof and while the view wasn't of a beautiful river valley at least he was able to see over many of the buildings around and had a horizon of sorts. An unusually strong gust of wind whipping over the edge of the roof drove him to seek shelter in the lee of the cement-walled shack housing the elevator. Somewhat protected from the menacing wind John turned his gaze upward. The air was too cold to hold moisture and, with the wind pushing away the pollution the local factories were constantly pumping into the air, the sky was crystal clear and the stars so brilliant John couldn't help but laugh in wonder. This was indeed a place he could come to for perspective.

He stood in silent marvel for some time. His body braced against the cold and his mind wandering beyond conscious thought, in silent unformed prayer. Time passed, minutes or hours he didn't know or care. The dog grew weary of the cold and of exploring and came and sat at his feet pulling John back to the present. He suddenly realized that he was ridiculously cold and that he had clarity in his thoughts he hadn't had in a long time. He still had frustrations and questions seemingly beyond measure but he knew beyond a shadow of a doubt that he was experiencing these things for a reason. The questions had meaning and a purpose. What if that crazy LiuPing was right? What if he had a story to tell and all these questions were meant to focus him on the real reason he was called to this place? To inspire and drive him to find answers or maybe to simply find the right questions? He looked back up at the star-filled blackness and spoke aloud into the icy wind.

"Lord, I don't know why you brought me to this place so far from home. We gave up everything we owned and the people we loved most to come here following your call and it has been so hard. I know I'm doing what you've called me to do but, I've never been so frustrated in my entire life and I don't know why. I know you never said following would be easy but, this doesn't make any sense to me. Please help me to make sense of it all. I know all this is happening for a reason. Please help me to see it."

The dog whined at his feet and looked up at John, tilting its head quizzically.

"It's ok Pengyou, I'm not going crazy," John laughed. "At least I don't think I am. Let's go in."

As John headed down the stairs he realized he was actually excited about going to the LiuPing Cafe again. He couldn't put his finger on why but he was pretty sure its crazy proprietor with his story was actually in some way sent to help him as unlikely as that might seem.

The next morning dawned bright and clear, usually a bad sign in winter meaning that it was going to be a bitter windy day. John woke up happy. After a leisurely breakfast with his wife and children, John bundled up and headed out the door promising he would be home soon and they would go play on the ice. He had a spring in his step as he headed up the street. Even the weather seemed to be cooperating to buoy his attitude as at 9:45 am it was already the warmest it had been in months with the temperature actually above freezing and the seemingly omnipresent wind strangely absent. Even when he arrived at the LiuPing Cafe and found the doors locked John stayed relatively upbeat. On the door was taped a note to: "California" that simply said; "I'll be a little late. Very important. You please wait." John headed back down the stairs, sat on the bottom one, and watched the world go by for a while wondering what, if any, insights today might bring.

"Hey California! You wait for me! Very happy to see you today!" LiuPing was beaming.

"I have to tell you, I'm actually very happy to see you today too!" John said with a smile of his own.

"Wa! So much progress we make already! Not so many question today... We may not even need to finish the story!" LiuPing laughed as they headed up the stairs.

"I wouldn't go that far," John laughed as he pulled off his jacket and settled into his now favorite chair. "I've just been thinking a lot about what you've said and I think there might be something to it. Maybe I do have a story to tell, or at least questions that need to be asked."

"Questions that need to be asked! Lots of those there are! But California, yesterday you were a mess... today, not so much. What has happened?" LiuPing didn't wait for an answer but went and busied himself behind the bar.

"Well, for starters, I found my own rooftop and I've been really thinking about one thing in particular that you asked yesterday."

"Wa! You see how important questions are? I ask one silly question and change your whole life! Ha ha! Which question was it California? Which question change your life? I have to remember it for next time!"

"I think it might be a bit soon to say that it's going to change my life," John chuckled. "But, it did make me think differently."

"That's the first step! Always need to change the way you think if you're going to change your life. We made good start then! But, what is the question?"

"Well, at one point yesterday you asked me how many of my troubles were caused by Ts'ang Chieh and, I've really been thinking about it. You're right, many of my frustrations, most of the frustrations in education today, wouldn't exist if writing hadn't been invented. In your story, The Master seems very wise and he must have ultimately decided that writing was a good thing... he allowed it to exist after all. He must have had a good reason to do so. I'm really looking forward to hearing more of the story and hearing why The Master decided it was a good thing despite his initial reservations. Maybe there is some ancient wisdom we have forgotten and could use in education today. Maybe that's the story I have to tell!"

LiuPing finished up at the bar, set the two steaming mugs of tea on the side table and settled into the chair next to John. He sat in silence with his eyes closed for a moment before turning and studying John with a thoughtful gaze.

"Very interesting...," was all he said for several long moments. "You now believe you may have a story to tell. That's great progress but, you still don't know what the story is. Plus, you are searching for answers in ancient wisdom... you may be even more frustrated before the story is over I think. We shall see."

"More frustrated? But..." John started but was quickly cut off.

"No questions now I think. When moving forward there is always a risk of frustrations. What if your assumptions are wrong? What if you are asking the wrong questions? What if, what if, what if? Always bad questions! Remember, right questions very important! Are you ready to hear more even if story causes more questions than it answers?"

Chastised, John sat nodding his head, a lopsided grin on his face.

EIGHT

"Ts'ang Chieh hurried through the night. It had been just two weeks since his disappointing visit to The Master and the urgent request to return immediately in the middle of the night with no explanation unsettled him. This was most unusual. The Master was well known as a night owl. He always said he did his best thinking when everyone was asleep. But, this was late even for him. With a sense of dread Ts'ang Chieh approached The Master's gates. Was The Master ill? Had there been an accident? Was The Master dead? Surely something terrible must have happened for Ts'ang Chieh to be called from his bed in the middle of this dark, dark night.

The Master's compound was completely dark. Ts'ang Chieh was quickly ushered into the house by one of the servants who told him he would find The Master on the roof. With just a touch of relief Ts'ang Chieh climbed the ladder to the rooftop sanctuary. If The Master was on the roof it probably meant that he wasn't sick and certainly wasn't dead.

On reaching the rooftop Ts'ang Chieh paused for a moment to let his eyes adjust to the darkness. The night was very still and the air crystal clear. There was no moon and the stars shone brighter than Ts'ang Chieh ever remembered them.

'Ts'ang Chieh my friend, is that you I hear? I'm sitting on the bench under the tree where we spoke last time you were here. Just follow the path lined with white stones and it will lead you right to me.'

'Yes master, it is I. I came as quickly as I could.'

Ts'ang Chieh carefully followed the path marked by white rocks glowing faintly in the starlight and soon found himself seated next to The Master under the incredible canopy of stars, which quite literally took his breath away.

'My young friend, thank you for coming so quickly in the middle on the night.' The Master said warmly. 'I'm sure you are wondering why I have sent for you but before I tell you there are a few questions I must ask you. I hope the questions will not make you too very uncomfortable.'

'You can ask me anything Master. I hide nothing from you.'

'Yes my young apprentice, I trust that is true. You have always been a loyal friend though sometimes a touch rash in your judgment. When you came here last, you shared your wonderfully creative new invention of characters. We discussed them at some length but needed more time to think through all the changes such a thing could bring to the world and if this was to be a good thing or a bad thing. You were disappointed, and rightly so as it is difficult to stop the excitement of genius. We agreed that for three weeks you would keep the characters a closely guarded secret and then we would meet again to discuss what would happen with your characters. Is all I have said how you remember what happened?'

'Yes Master, that is exactly what happened,' Ts'ang Chieh replied confused.

'Excellent! Now my young friend, I must ask; what has become of your characters?'

'Master, I did just as you asked me. Paopao and I wrapped up the characters so no one could see them and we took them to my home and hid them. We spoke to no one on the way home though great crowds were constantly badgering us with questions. Yes, I remember I was quite bothered by all the questions but, for once doing something right, Paopao was able to get the people to stop pestering us. I don't know what he said but it was most effective. I was grateful to him.'

'Ah, very good! I assume you've spoken to no one about the characters since then?'

'Of course not Master.'

'And your characters, you put them in a secret spot? They are still carefully hidden?'

'Yes Master, I haven't even looked at them myself since I had Paopao hide them and I've given Paopao three weeks of rest so he hasn't been around to disturb them either.'

'I see. So, do you know where Paopao hid them? Are you sure they are safe?'

Ts'ang Chieh was momentarily taken aback.

'Well, no I don't actually know where they were hidden. I was so tired and Paopao had been so helpful I gladly accepted his help when he offered it. Master, you wouldn't have called me out here in the middle of the night for no reason. Has something happened?'

'Yes Ts'ang Chieh, I'm afraid it looks like something terrible may have happened, something which is going to take a tremendous amount of work and wisdom to fix.' The Master said gently. 'My young friend, I don't know for certain yet but, it appears that young foolish Paopao has decided to try and make a name for himself by stealing your characters and selling the knowledge of them. I'm afraid he is doing irreversible harm as great care needs to be taken when giving something as powerful as your characters to the people. The people must be properly prepared and shown how to be careful with new tools and I know Paopao has neither the patience nor wisdom to do that.'

Ts'ang Chieh was torn between bitter searing anger at Paopao and paralyzing fear at what might happen. How could they undo the damage Paopao had done?

'Master, what will we do?'

'First, we must find Paopao, see if he has indeed done what we fear and, if so, stop him. I and a few servants will take care of finding him. In the meantime, you start thinking of how we could best mitigate the damage he has caused. It won't be easy. You'll stay here in my home until we get this straightened out. I think we will need to speak often but for now, let's get some rest. We will talk again after the morning meal. Meet me here.'

Ts'ang Chieh had a restless night. He had tossed and turned for hours unable to fall asleep. When he did finally drift off he dreamed of the phoenix bird. It was taunting him. The morning meal passed in a blur and when he finally sat down beside The Master on the roof he had far more questions than he had answers.

'Ah my friend, you look like you did not rest well. Was your bed not comfortable?' The Master looked fully rested and full of energy though Ts'ang Chieh was sure he had gotten even less sleep than he had. The Master handed Ts'ang Chieh a mug of his special tea. 'You must get enough sleep! It's very hard to think properly when your mind is not rested!'

'I know Master, I tried. The bed was very comfortable but the spinning of my mind would not stop.'

'Yes, yes, I understand it is sometimes impossible to sleep when one's mind wants to wrestle with something. Sometimes it's better to not fight it. You can always sleep later.'

'Master, one thing that kept going over and over through my mind was a question. Is this really a bad thing? I don't fully understand why it must be.'

'Hmmm, that is an excellent question. Good or bad, only time will tell. It is what it is. But, we can ask, is it the best thing? And if not, what can we do to make it better.'

'But how Master? We can't undo what Paopao has done. We don't even know yet for sure if what we suspect is true.'

'Aiya, that is true. My most reliable servants are searching for the rascal and I'm certain we will have our answers soon. In the meantime, let us discuss why it's important to prepare the people for new tools and why we must do so. Let us also decide what the very best way to teach the people would be. Then, when we know for sure if your invention has been unleashed we may have a better understanding of how to undo any damage Paopao has caused and help people learn how to use it. If we find that Paopao is innocent, our time will not have been wasted because we will be ready to introduce the people to your powerful new tool ourselves.'

'That is a very wise plan Master. Before we begin, may I ask one more question? Last night you kept calling my characters powerful. You did it again just now. I don't understand. They are just symbols. They can't even physically do anything. Why are they so powerful?'

'Ah, they are powerful in a different way, in a way we have never seen in the world before. Your characters have the power to make people think. Not just think either, they have the power to make people think very specific thoughts... The exact thoughts the person who laid out the order of the characters wanted them to think. For example, you used them to force me to think "What makes a fish a fish?" I didn't plan to think about a fish. I didn't even want to think about a fish but, you made me. Never before has man had the power to force someone else to think exactly the thoughts he wanted them to. Very, very powerful! And, not just as a tool I think but a weapon as well.'

Ts'ang Chieh was astonished. He had never dreamed that his creation could have this kind of power. Never even considered that it could be a powerful weapon. But, The Master was right. It did truly have this power.

'I am such a fool for not seeing this Master. I am ashamed. I only saw the good things that this tool could do and didn't even see its full awesome potential. I was so excited and I failed to keep it safe and hidden because I didn't see it for what it truly was.'

'No my friend, you are not a fool. It took great wisdom to invent this but, as I said weeks ago, the inventor is often too closely attached to his work to be able to see the entire picture. This is good actually. If it were not so, if every inventor were to see in advance all the consequences of their creations, no one would ever have the courage to invent anything. What you have created is a marvel. I know that together we can use what wisdom we have to take whatever steps are needed to make all of this better.'

'How do we begin Master?'

'Before deciding how to use a new tool one must first examine what one believes and what they hold most dear. They must focus on what their goal in the very end is and then, and only then, they can start to plan just how to use the tool to help reach their goal. If you don't start this way, if you start instead with the tool, you will find many uses for the tool but many of them may go directly against the goal you are trying to achieve. For example, one of the boards on my front door is loose. It is something so easy to fix a child could do it but, if I simply handed that child there in the yard a hammer, would my door get fixed? Of course not even though that hammer would be used to pound on many things. But, if I were to explain first what I wanted the child to be able to accomplish with the hammer and then gave it to him, my door would most likely be fixed. So, we start there. What do we believe? When you first described your invention to me you claimed we would be able to capture and pass down all the knowledge and wisdom of our age. So, what do we believe about knowledge and wisdom and how are they best acquired? And then, what is our goal? What do we want our people to learn and how do we want them to learn it?'

'Those are huge questions Master and I'm not sure I have all the answers. You have questioned my wisdom many times. If I can't grow in wisdom myself how can I know how best to help others acquire it?'

'Yes my friend, these may be some of the biggest questions but, the power of your creation requires them. Let's start simpler maybe? How about we first ask what is the difference between wisdom and knowledge?'

'Well, I'd say knowledge is knowing the facts about something. Wisdom is a bit harder to describe. I think it is often thought of as knowing what to do at a given time but, I think there is more to it. It's almost like someone with wisdom has a deeper knowledge of something and that makes it look like they know what to do at a given time.'

'Ah, yes I think you are going the right direction. I've heard it said that wisdom is not just knowing about something but knowing of something. Very good! Now, how does one acquire each of them? Let's start with knowledge.'

Ts'ang Chieh thought for a long moment, 'That's not such a hard question really. One can get knowledge through many ways, by being shown something, by observing, or simply because someone told you something they had knowledge of. Knowledge is quite easy to get really, it seems to be most everywhere.'

'Good, I agree knowledge seems to be almost everywhere if one would just open one's eyes or reach out their hands to take it. People can even give knowledge to each other easily. Such a simple silly thing really. Sure it has some value but too much of it can weigh one down and how much of it is truly useful for anything? What about wisdom? Can people just give it to one another?'

'Well, people certainly can't give it to each other, in fact, it seems like attempting to give wisdom to someone else makes it even harder for them to accept it. It seems most people refuse it when you offer it to them. Sometimes they even get quite upset about it.'

'Truer words have never been spoken!' The Master laughed a hearty laugh that left him with a coughing fit. 'Then how does one get it?'

'I'm afraid I can't say I know for sure how one gets it. It seems like one day one doesn't have it and the next, there it is. Older people seem to have more of it than the young but, I'm pretty sure the passing of time isn't what causes it for I've seen plenty of foolish old men and also a good number of young men who have shown wisdom far beyond their years. I'm beginning to think it has something to do with the experiences one has in life but, I think there is something more to it than that.'

'Yes there is more to wisdom than just the passing of time of... experience. I'd say to acquire wisdom it takes testing knowledge against experience and vice-versa and learning from it. This is what gives wisdom that deeper knowledge feeling. I'd say a good portion of wisdom is made up of knowledge that has been tested and proven over time through experience. To acquire wisdom one must take the time to reflect on what they think they know and what they have experienced and search for the truth in it. This is why some never gain wisdom... they never stop and think and learn anything from their actions. Do you understand this?'

'Yes Master thank you for explaining what I could not. I understand far more fully now as I can see what I was missing.'

'Wonderful but, your understanding now does disprove something you said earlier! It is actually possible to give someone wisdom by leading them to it, if they are willing to follow. But, I think even then it must be tested by some prior experience the person had for them to be so willing. Interesting, I must think more on this later. Now, a question to see what you've learned; you claimed your characters would be able to pass on all the knowledge and wisdom of our age. Do you still believe that is true?'

'We have established that it is very easy to pass knowledge to another so I have no doubt that it can be done with characters though some of the knowledge may be of little use. Wisdom is a much harder question. I think it would be easy to record wisdom in characters but, wisdom is much harder to pass on. If the person who sees the wisdom in the characters is willing to accept it then it could be quite easy. It seems impossible that someone unwilling or inexperienced would gain wisdom from seeing it in characters. Though, I wonder... what if the viewing of the characters was combined with some experience? Could that make the person willing to accept the wisdom in them? What if the experience was marked down in characters along with the wisdom itself? We've already discovered that one can cause another to think specific thoughts through characters. I wonder if that experience alone could be enough?'

'That is a most excellent question! I believe you are running down the path of wisdom far ahead of me. Give an old man a chance to catch up a moment!'

They sat together in the shade, Ts'ang Chieh staring off at the horizon, his mind spinning. The Master sat perfectly still with his eyes closed. He was still for so long Ts'ang Chieh thought he must have drifted off to sleep. He was after all a very old man. No sooner had Ts'ang Chieh thought this than The Master spoke startling him.

'I think you may be correct. One could certainly pass on wisdom if the recipient was willing to accept it when they saw it. I think that one could also pass on the experience needed to accept new wisdom if the person laying out the characters is skilled in telling a story and making others think the necessary thoughts. It would not be easy though. I think it would be far more likely that people would skip right over the wisdom in their quest for knowledge and end up overloaded with knowledge while actually losing wisdom. Certainly it would be a worthy goal. Ah, that brings up the other big question. What is our goal?'

'Well, now that we have thought through so much, I don't know that this is such a hard question. We want our people to learn the knowledge that they need but what we really want is for them to grow in wisdom.'

'You are indeed growing my young friend. Today we have made great progress! Now we must decide if your characters are a useful tool in reaching that goal and if so, how can they best be used? Or, should we decide to keep them hidden and not use them at all?'

At that moment they heard a great commotion outside the gates. As they turned to look across the courtyard to the source of the trouble, in walked two of The Master's servants with Paopao sandwiched between them. One look at his face, even from this great distance told them The Master's last question was moot."

NINE

"So California, what do you think? Did Paopao steal the characters?"

"Well, to be honest I was so focused on other parts of the story I almost forgot about Paopao. He seems almost irrelevant."

"Aiya, Paopao not irrelevant! Nothing in this story irrelevant! You think I want to waste my holiday time with irrelevant. You will see, Paopao become very important to the story!" LiuPing paused and took a sip of his long cold tea. "But you're right, today Paopao not very important! Ha ha!"

John shook his head and got up to stretch his legs. He walked over to the sliding doors that opened out onto the roof and stared out at the horizon. LiuPing made himself busy making more tea.

"You know, this story isn't exactly going the way I thought it would," John said as he crossed the room and sat at the ornate bar. "I'm not sure The Master would have allowed the characters to be used if it weren't for Paopao."

"Ha! Now that is irrelevant! We know what happened. Don't waste any more time on the what-if questions! I warned you that you might get more frustrated before the end. Focus on the important parts! What spoke to you today?"

"Well, there was so much. I'm really going to have to think about it for a while before I really understand it all. First, there was all that stuff about writing having the power to make people think specific thoughts... I've never heard that before, never thought about it. That is a very powerful thing! I guess that's why they say the pen is mightier than the sword. With a sword you can control someone's body but with a pen... You can control their mind! Maybe only for as long as it takes them to read what you wrote, but still! That's power!"

"Yes, power indeed but, does that help you?"

"I don't know. It actually brings up a whole crop of new questions though."

"Save the questions for later. For now let's just focus on what you heard. What else caught your attention?"

"I really liked the concept of knowing what your beliefs and goals are before deciding to use a new tool. That seems totally opposite from how we usually do it today. Sometimes it seems people today create tools to solve problems that don't exist which then create problems they don't have tools for. It sure would be nice to have some clear focus at times."

"Yes, that's wonderful! What else?"

"The whole knowledge vs. wisdom part was interesting. In education we seem to focus entirely on knowledge but The Master and Ts'ang Chieh almost seem to look down on knowledge. They certainly don't think it's hard to get... that kind of goes against the major philosophies of education today. It even seems like they were saying too much knowledge can be a bad thing. It's strange you know. We want our students to be wise, I mean, who wouldn't but, I don't think I've ever been in an education class or a professional development training or conference where we have ever mentioned wisdom. It certainly isn't focused on. We just kind of hope they get it without ever even defining what it is."

"Do you think that is a good thing?"

"I don't really know. Good thing, bad thing, it is what it is. In education today we focus on things we can measure. Knowledge can be measured, wisdom can't."

"But, which is more important?"

"Aghh! That's not fair! I'm already frustrated because there are too many things I have to weave together and many of them aren't measurable. I can't add another one!"

"Is it really so important that everything be measurable?" LiuPing smiled gently.

"Everyone in education today sure seems to think so. Measurable standards and data are the very driving force behind public education back home. I thought coming here and working in a Christian school maybe things would be different. But no, we have adopted the same ultramodern philosophy of education. I don't really think that is bad though. After all, it's important to be able to measure ones results. If you don't, how do you know if the students are learning?"

"Ah yes, very important to know that your students are learning! Knowledge is important today. So, maybe that is one of your values... Knowledge is more important today than wisdom!"

"Aghh! I'm not saying that!"

"Well California, you might not want to say it but that's what you're describing! Unless you have a new way to measure wisdom. Measurable, measurable, measurable."

"I understand what you're saying but you just don't understand what it's like in education today. It is so hard to integrate something that can't be measured with something that can. We try to do that with Biblical principles and, well, it just gets frustrating. The kids just pick out the little pieces of the Bible we try to integrate into our lessons and just puppet them back to us and forget them. It's not becoming part of who they are as people. Now add wisdom on top of all that? Impossible! Even in your story they are almost saying that wisdom can't be taught!"

"Aiya, they say no such thing. Difficult? Yes! But not impossible! You will see I think. Maybe you need to step back to get a different perspective?"

"I don't know if that will help. I've been studying this for so long, from so many different perspectives I'm not sure what to think anymore."

"Yes, you see! That's what the story warns about... too much knowledge! You have so much knowledge you can't see the big picture anymore. Forget what you know and think about what you believe. Who knows, it might help!"

John just shook his head in frustration.

"If Ts'ang Chieh and The Master figured it out I'd sure love to hear it!" he said with a sigh.

"See, I told you this story would make you more frustrated before it was over! I think maybe this enough talking for today. Go home and rest California. Think about things. Come back tomorrow... 10am. We talk more then. Maybe stay whole day!"

John bundled up for the walk home but when he stepped out onto the sidewalk he smiled, untied his scarf and partially unzipped his jacket.

Maybe spring would come after all! The mere thought of a day when he wouldn't have to wear so many layers he could hardly move his arms seemed impossible but, maybe, just maybe. He was so enraptured with the mere thought of the freedom of shorts and a tee-shirt he nearly didn't think the entire way home.

That evening, after an afternoon of playing out on the pond with his children, John found himself back up on the roof with Pengyou. Haze hung in the air obscuring the stars but there was no wind and the air was much warmer than the night before. John felt he had so much to think about that he frankly didn't know where to start. He stood in silence for a moment looking to where the stars would have been.

"You know this was difficult enough without you throwing wisdom into the mix!" he prayed aloud. "Seriously, I already have to figure out how to deal with standards and benchmarks and school-wide learning results and Biblical integration and now wisdom too? How am I supposed to do this?" As soon as the words left his lips a single unbidden thought clear and sharp as crystal flashed through his mind.

"It's simple, you're just missing something."

John stood for a moment stunned by the clarity of the thought, rolling it over in his mind.

"That's not helping!" he said into the misty night. Of course he was missing something. He was probably missing a lot of somethings. Knowing that didn't help one bit. Still the thought remained lodged in his consciousness un-wielding.

He forcefully pushed the thought aside and thought back to LiuPing's admonition to forget what he knew and think about what he believed... whatever that meant. He knew what he believed and he believed what he knew. There was way too much to think about with what he believed and what he knew for this ever to be simple despite what that voice stuck in his head said. He couldn't see how adding one more thing, whatever that something he was missing was, could possibly make any of this simpler. Scooping up Pengyou he headed back downstairs as frustrated as he had been in a long time.

The next day, John almost didn't go to the LiuPing cafe. He didn't want to think about it anymore. He was just about ready to throw in the towel. In the end he found himself standing at the base of that familiar dark stairwell because he knew LiuPing would be there, because he knew for some reason LiuPing cared enough to give up his holiday in order to tell him a story. What a strange fellow he was. Upon reaching the door he found LiuPing was already there waiting for him, mug of tea in hand seemingly raring to go.

"Good morning California! So happy to see you today! We make so much progress yesterday. Very excited to see what today bring!" LiuPing was excited. It annoyed John.

"You think we made progress? I was so frustrated last night I almost didn't come today!"

"Ah, but you did come! Very good! Frustrated doesn't mean no progress! Sometime it takes frustration to drive progress. Yes, frustration is like questions... leads to answers!"

"You certainly have a way of twisting things into something good." John laughed. "I hope my frustration leads to answers soon!"

"Probably not today California, probably not today but, let's see what we can learn."

TEN

"The Master's servants had tied Paopao's hands and feet and tethered him to a pole in the courtyard. He was tied to the top of the pole in such a way that he couldn't lower his tied hands below his shoulders, he couldn't sit, and it was hard to balance with his ankles lashed together. He had been left out in the mid-day sun for only an hour but to him it seemed like he had been there forever. He was whimpering softly as The Master and Ts'ang Chieh approached followed by two of The Master's servants carrying wicked looking whips. The four encircled Paopao and stood in ominous silence. It was more than he could bear.

'Master! Forgive me!' Paopao screamed to Ts'ang Chieh. 'I am a wicked wicked servant and stole a great treasure from you but please, show mercy!'

The Master stepped closer to Paopao. He spoke quietly, calmly. 'What are you talking about Paopao? What is this great treasure you are speaking of? What have you done?'

'Master Ts'ang Chieh ordered me to hide the characters he created. He trusted me but I...'

'Go on Paopao.'

'He trusted me but, I took the characters and have been teaching them to people for money.'

'How many people Paopao?' The Master was still utterly calm which only served to frighten Paopao more.

'Many, many people.'

The Master smiled, "Paopao, this is indeed a very wicked thing you have done. You have not only broken your master Ts'ang Chieh's trust but you have stolen from him. Even worse, you have stolen from all our people. Do you understand this?'

'Master, I understand I have wronged master Ts'ang Chieh and for this I am sorry and surely deserving of punishment but, I don't understand how I have stolen from all our people.'

'Paopao, for all of history our people have shared knowledge freely. It has never been something to be cheapened by being bought or sold. In selling this knowledge to the people you have taken money from them for something that should have been free for the taking. You have stolen something that belonged to them as surely as if you had threatened them with a weapon and taken their money by force. This in itself is a terrible thing but I fear that there is an even greater damage you have caused. Now the people know that knowledge itself may have value... monetary value. I'm afraid of what could come of this. I'm afraid people may stop freely sharing knowledge, hoarding it and only sharing it for money, afraid this will make knowledge seem more valuable than it is, making it seem more valuable than wisdom. On top of all this Paopao, you have stolen and shared Master Ts'ang Chieh's characters... which unfortunately could make this hoarding and selling of knowledge even easier! Yes Paopao, I'm afraid you have done great harm to the future of our very way of life. I don't know if in the history of the world someone has done something as potentially wicked as what you have done.' He paused and pulled a long, thin, sinister looking knife from his belt. 'Your punishment will be most severe.'

As The Master stepped toward him Paopao turned ghost white, too frightened even to scream. The Master reached him in two measured steps, reached up with the knife and cut the cord tethering Paopao to the pole. 'You get to help figure out how to fix this.' The Master said softly as Paopao collapsed into his arms.

Turning Paopao over to his servants he ordered, 'Take him into the house and place him in the most comfortable guest room available. When he awakes give him all he desires to eat and drink. When he is satisfied, have him bathe and dress him in comfortable new clothes. Be sure that no one mistreats him in the slightest but don't allow him to leave the house. Master Ts'ang Chieh and I will speak with him this evening on the rooftop."

"Wait a minute," John exclaimed. "This guy steals and sells something that doesn't belong to him, something that could disrupt their entire society, and they're treating him like a king? What's wrong with these people?"

"What do you mean? He's being punished." LiuPing smiled.

"Doesn't sound much like punishment to me... comfortable room, good food, new clothes. Shoot, he's being waited on hand and foot. Sounds more like a vacation. I'd take that punishment any day."

"Maybe you already have California, maybe you already have. That's why you are so frustrated...!"

"What?"

"Aiya California, it so simple. Paopao is trapped in a cage. Sure it is comfortable cage but, aiya still a cage. He has to help fix a big problem... how to teach the people. No, even bigger problem... how to teach the people in a way that will lead them down a different path than they are likely to choose on their own. You see any similarities?"

"I guess when you put it that way, I do feel trapped and I am trying to find a solution to a similar problem. But, I'm not being punished. No one is making me do this!"

"Interesting, very interesting. I would ask, 'Why are you doing this?' but, that's not the right question and trying to answer it won't help us. The fact is, there is a reason and whatever that reason may be, you are doing it and I believe it needs doing. Shall I continue the story?"

John simply nodded and stared down into the bottom of his tea mug as if it somehow held the key.

"Evening found Paopao on his hands and knees kowtowing before The Master and Ts'ang Chieh.

'Masters please forgive your worthless servant! I am not worthy of the kindness you have shown me this afternoon for I deserve to be punished. I'm afraid that your kindness will show itself to be a cruel joke and my punishment will be even harsher because of it. Oh please, please have mercy on me!'

'Get up you silly boy,' ordered Ts'ang Chieh. 'The Master has already told you what your punishment will be! Be grateful it was not in my hands!'

'Yes, I have indeed,' agreed The Master. 'However Paopao, you may be correct. Your punishment may truly seem too harsh before this is over. I have shown you more kindness than you deserve and I will continue to do so because you are going to need all the strength you can muster. You will need to be well fed and rested for the task ahead of you and you are not to leave my courtyard. If you do you will be caught and the mercy I have shown you will be forfeit. Do you understand what's expected of you?'

'I'm not certain Master. I seem to remember you saying I will help figure out how to fix this but, I guess I don't really know what is to be fixed or why you say it will be so hard. It seems very simple to me. I just need to give the characters back to Master Ts'ang so they can be hidden again and return the money to the people. Isn't that enough?'

'Paopao, earlier I explained to you how what you did would have effects far beyond today. I don't believe what you've done can simply be undone. No, I'm afraid that characters and their unwanted side effects are going to be with us for a very long time. From this day hence knowledge will be worth gold and ideas once freely shared will be hoarded, bought, and sold. This can't be stopped. There is one thing we may be able to do... we will try to find a way to use the characters so that the people will still value wisdom over knowledge. We must find a way to teach people, using characters, that preserves our traditions, values and wisdom so that our people can truly grow, not just be stuffed full of empty knowledge. This is no easy task. Fortunately, Master Ts'ang and I have already spoken much about this and will be here to help guide your thoughts.'

'But Master, I am young and not nearly as wise as my masters. I don't even know where to begin. What do I do?'

'Well young one, you may not be as wise but, you do possess one particular bit of knowledge that your masters do not. You have shown the characters to people. You must have devised some way to teach them or no one would have paid you. That's where we will start, but not tonight. I want you to go and rest and think about how you taught the people. What things did you think about while doing it? What was so important that it had to be passed on and what was the best way to do so? Yes, you have much to think about. You go and organize your thoughts and we will speak again tomorrow evening.'

As Paopao rose and headed down to his room Ts'ang Chieh spoke. 'Master, do you really think it is wise to include Paopao in this? He is nothing but a foolish boy and this will be a hard enough task for us without having to watch him every moment. I don't see what he could possibly add that will help us.'

'Ah Master Ts'ang, I share your fears but who can know for sure. Paopao may yet be useful if only by simply telling us his ideas so that we know what to avoid and don't waste time on foolish paths ourselves.' The Master laughed, his voice echoing across the courtyard startling the chickens. 'I will say Ts'ang Chieh, this is looking like it could keep us diverted for some time. I just love a challenge!'

The next day as Paopao sat looking forlornly out his window staining to think of a way to make how he was teaching sound insightful and so impress his masters, Ts'ang Chieh and The Master walked about the village discussing and rejecting their own thoughts. They even walked along the river to the place Ts'ang Chieh had discovered the track's of the Fenghuang on that fateful day, hoping to find some inspiration there. As they settled into their accustomed perch on the roof at the end of the day they agreed that they hadn't made a lot of forward progress but they had rejected a lot of bad ideas... progress in a way.

As the sun set casting its final rays over the limestone peaks rimming the valley making the whole world red, golden and warm, Paopao joined them looking quite worse than he had the day before. He wasn't accustomed to spending an entire day in thought and the strain of it was clear.

'Good evening Master Ts'ang, Master FuXia.'

'Good evening Paopao, I trust you've had a productive day?' Ts'ang Chieh replied with much more kindness in his voice than he felt.

'Oh yes Master, I spent the entire day thinking about how I taught people your characters. I have remembered much and hope I can be helpful!'

'As do we!' The Master said joining in the conversation with a smile. 'So young one, what can you tell us about teaching with this new thing? How did you approach it? What did you do?'

'Master, today I struggled with those same questions. It was hard for me because, well, truly I didn't think of them before starting to teach. I didn't know that they were important. I was just focused on giving the people the knowledge of the characters and taking their money. To be honest, I don't even know that I really taught them anything. I just showed them the characters and told them the meaning behind each and left them to figure the rest out on their own. I guess I figured that they were mostly good, intelligent people who could just as well explore the characters on their own and decide for themselves what was useful, what was true. I just kind of set the stage for them to explore and guided them as little as I could.'

'That is most interesting Paopao. You said you didn't think about any of this before starting to teach, didn't think that it was important.

Do you still think that way now that you've had some time to reflect? Is there anything you would go back and change?'

'I think your questions are very important but I'm not sure I know why. I wish I could go back and redo everything. I'd leave those blasted characters on the cart and leave it to you and Master Ts'ang to figure out!'

'Yes Paopao, I believe you would!' The Master laughed. 'But, since you're now stuck figuring this out with us let's look at what you were doing a little closer and see if we can learn anything from it. I think the first thing that struck me is how you viewed your learners. You described them as mostly good and intelligent and thought that if they simply explored on their own they could discover or create their own knowledge. Does that sound correct?'

'Yes Master, and I still think they are good people and they did a wonderful job of discovering things! They made connection I hadn't seen before. They truly learned a lot.'

'Interesting. Master Ts'ang, what do you think?'

'Well, it is interesting and I think Paopao has hit on one important truth... Learning is an active process. However, just because people are good doesn't mean they will always come up with the right answers on their own. I'm certain people love to explore, it's exciting. But, it's very easy to get lost venturing into new places if you don't have someone to guide you. Also, bear in mind that right now we're really only talking about knowledge. If our goal is wisdom I think having the proper guide is even more important. If someone creates their own knowledge and it turns out to be incorrect that is a bad thing but how much worse would it be if, in the quest for wisdom, they create their own truth that is false? Their own morality?'

'Excellent points Ts'ang Chieh! I think you are correct. While there are some good things about this approach I'm afraid in the end it simply relies entirely too much on the perception of the learner.'

At these words Paopao's head drooped and he stared at the ground in shame. He had failed.

'Paopao, we are proud of the thinking you did today. You very clearly told us all we needed to know about how you taught Master Ts'ang's characters and, for not having thought about how to teach beforehand I think you did a fine job. We have learned something today from your experience and that will help us move forward. Because of you we can see the power of exploration and know that learning is indeed an active process. Well done!' The Master smiled.

'I thank you Master. I thought I had failed, again,' he paused, hopeful. 'Am I free to go now?'

'Oh Paopao, we have only just begun and I'm afraid you will be with us every step of the way. It will likely take a very long time. I want you to go and think more. I want you to think about what you could do differently to guide your learners. Remember, we want to focus not just on knowledge but on wisdom. There must be absolutes to help guide the learners. We can't just have them walking down a dark path all alone waiting to get lost. Can you do that?'

'Yes Master, I will try though I'm not even sure where to start. This may take days.'

'Yes Paopao, maybe even weeks. Go and rest now. We will talk again in a few days.'

After Paopao left The Master and Ts'ang Chieh sat staring out at the moonlit horizon each lost in their own thoughts before getting up in silence and heading down to bed themselves."

ELEVEN

LiuPing's story was interrupted by a knock at the cafe's locked main door. He jumped up from his seat and scurried across the room to open the door. "I decided to order lunch and have it delivered for us. I hope you are hungry!"

John watched as LiuPing started to unpack the bag the delivery boy had given him. There were only three dishes. John could only recognize one... soup, delivered in a plastic bag. He wasn't sure he'd ever get used to seeing soup packaged that way. It just seemed wrong, asking for trouble. The second dish consisted of thin strips of meat, onions, peppers, and what looked like flat-bread all fried together with what looked like a seriously excessive amount of seasoning. It smelled wonderful. John stared dubiously at the third dish. It looked like a textural nightmare. This dish looked to be simply a plate of very over-cooked green beans with an equal amount of whole peppercorns, a bit of some fried, ground mystery meat, and strips of something extremely slimy looking which John couldn't identify.

"Don't worry California, I won't poison you! Try it, you'll like it! That dish called naan rou char, lamb and nan bread fried together, very tasty. The other dish gan bing dou jou. It's green beans with Sichuan peppercorn...what some call numbing spice but I have them add something special... eggplant! Turns a good dish into a great dish."

John decided he really had nothing to lose. The lamb dish was excellent and though he found the numbing sensation of the peppercorns in the bean dish a bit strange it was one of the best things he had ever eaten. " Wow, this is really good!"

"I told you! You can trust LiuPing, especially about food!"

"Alright, alright," John laughed, "I admit you know a thing or two about food... and drinks! I'll give you that but... I'm still not certain your story is going anywhere, at least not anywhere that's going to help me. Is it ever going to give me any answers?"

"Aiya, California! Story is not about answers, it about making you think."

"But, I thought you said I was thinking too much already? Isn't that what all this is about... I listen to your story and in the end you tell me some ancient secret, truth, wisdom, whatever, that will answer all my questions?"

"Ah, if that's what you're looking for you are going to be disappointed. I'm not telling you this story in order to answer your questions. I'm hoping it will help you ask the right questions... remember? The answers at the end of this story may not be what you're looking for."

"I know, I know, I was just hoping maybe you were joking about that. The story has made me think about things a bit differently so far... hasn't helped my frustration at all but, maybe you're right. Maybe the frustration will be a good thing in the end."

"Good attitude California! I think maybe you are starting to think little differently."

"Maybe I am. I think taking the time to stop and think things through and get a bigger perspective is starting to help."

"Yes, yes, it helps to see the big picture but, you also must remember to not over-think things too. See it big but, keep it simple! We should continue the story. I want to try and finish it soon, before I take a short vacation. Ok?"

"Carry on my sage. I'd love to hear the end of this story."

"So, The Master was right, it took Paopao nearly two weeks to think of a better way to teach. Every day he stayed shut-up in his room, only coming out to eat and take short breaks tinkering with things in The Master's workshop to clear his mind. He struggled mightily because he truly wanted to please The Master. He was hopeful that he would find the solution to this problem and earn his way back into The Master's good graces.

Each day while Paopao agonized alone in his room Ts'ang Chieh and The Master met and talked together. Some days they wandered the countryside. Others were spent entirely on the rooftop. Always they talked, planned, debated. They were in high spirits as each loved to solve problems and they truly enjoyed working together. They were making fine progress.

Finally Paopao felt he was ready to share. He approached The Master over the morning meal and they agreed to meet that evening on the rooftop. Paopao spent the day once more thinking through his plan so that he was sure to be ready.

Evening came and Paopao found Ts'ang Chieh and The Master in their accustomed place on the roof watching the last of the sunset linger over the valley.

'Good evening my masters.'

'Good evening Paopao,' Ts'ang Chieh replied warmly. He was somewhat amazed that Paopao was still around and even more amazed that his lazy wicked servant actually seemed to be taking this project seriously. Ts'ang Chieh had never seen Paopao work so diligently. Maybe there was hope for him after all.

'So Paopao, you have finished? Tell us your plan and we can discuss it,' The Master ordered.

'Masters, I have thought long and hard about my plan and what you told me and I have made a lot of changes. I see that I was relying too much on the learners before. I made too many assumptions about what they knew and about what they could learn without guidance. In my new plan I make no such assumptions. My entire view of the learners has changed. I now assume that they know nothing. They are simply empty wineskins to be filled and shaped by what I teach them. I have made it so that the person teaching, in this case me, is the authority and all the students will learn comes from me. I have taken all I think they should learn, the facts and skills, and put it in a logical sequence. I'll use this sequence to guide what I teach. I will teach them to think by focusing on logic and reason relying on the facts they have learned. It will all be very disciplined.'

'That is very interesting Paopao, very different from your last approach. But tell me, how will you know if your students have learned with this approach?' The Master asked.

'Ah that is the beauty of my new plan Master. Since I have taken all they will learn and put it in order it is very easy to simply test them at the end of each section and see if they remember the information. If they remember it all they have learned. If not, they have failed. I will reward those who learn and punish those who fail. The competition for rewards will push them to learn more, faster.'

Ts'ang Chieh shook his head bewildered. 'So, you are going to be relying on them memorizing a sequence of facts while "focusing on logic and reason" and you are going to test them somehow to see if they remember it all. You are also going to make this competitive. Does that pretty much sum up this new plan?'

'Yes Master, in this way everyone will learn the same thing. It doesn't depend on whether or not the student explores and doesn't require them to make up their own, maybe faulty, knowledge. All they will need to know will be provided to them and they just need to take it in. Isn't it wonderful?' Paopao beamed.

'Aiya Paopao. Didn't we agree that learning was an active process? Weren't we concerned that our people will grow in wisdom? Here you have made a plan that completely leaves out both of these important things.' Ts'ang Chieh shook his head.

'But Masters, you said that there must be absolutes... that the learners couldn't just figure things out for themselves as my first plan allowed. They needed to be guided. Isn't that what I've done?'

The Master looked kindly at Paopao. 'Yes Paopao, that is what you've done but, I'm afraid you've gone too far. This new plan is almost completely the opposite of your first plan. You've lost most of what was good in it. I know this is incredibly hard but I want you to try one more time. Try to find a plan in the middle, keeping what is best from each. Do you think you can do this Paopao?'

'I don't know Master but I will try. It may take some time.'

'Then you should get started right away. Be sure to let us know how you are progressing.'

After Paopao had returned to his room downstairs Ts'ang Chieh and The Master sat in silence each contemplating what they had just heard. Ts'ang Chieh was the first to break the silence.

'Master, I'm not sure we are gaining anything by tormenting Paopao this way. This task is simply beyond him and taking the time to entertain his ideas could be better used discussing our own.'

'You may be right my friend. We gained precious little from him tonight but still I think he may have some further role to play before this is all over. Even though he is going over ground you and I have already rejected as being the wrong path to wisdom, he did have a couple unique points I hadn't considered for example, competition. Is it a good thing? Could or should it be used to motivate people to learn? This is an interesting question. His new view of the learner was different as well. How did he put it? Oh yes, an empty wine skin to be filled and shaped by what is taught. This is interesting imagery I wouldn't have thought Paopao was capable of. I don't think he had it quite right though... wine may fill a bag and thereby alter its shape but that shape is still constrained by the design of its creator. No amount of filling can change it beyond a certain point as the wine will simply pour out when the skin is stretched full or, the wineskin will burst. I wonder if it's the same with people and knowledge... they can only hold so much? What about wisdom? I'd like to think that it has more power to transform and I hope there is no limit to the amount one person can contain. Fascinating isn't it? And to think, I may have never thought about this if it weren't for foolish young Paopao.'

'I guess it's true that wisdom can be found everywhere, even in the most foolish of things, if one takes the time to look for it,' Ts'ang Chieh allowed.

'Yes, it seems the wise can find wisdom in everything mainly I think because they are intently focused on seeking it out. They are on a constant hunt for wisdom and truth. That's what we want our people to become, people who long for wisdom and truth, not hoarders of knowledge. Let us not lose that focus ourselves.'

'Master, I think we are well on the way to having some of the answers we are looking for.'

'Yes Ts'ang Chieh my friend, I can feel it too. Isn't this a wonderfully exciting time? I am truly enjoying working with you."

The sudden eruption of "The Flight of the Bumblebees" full blast from LiuPing's cell phone caused both to jump, John nearly upending his tea mug. LiuPing hurriedly answered it, said a few short phrases in Chinese John couldn't understand the words of but the urgency was evident.

"Aiya! There are problems with travel arrangements for my trip. So sorry California, I have to go. You go now, think about today's stories, about focus. Come back tomorrow, 10 o'clock, we finish story then ok?"

Before John could even respond he had been scurried out the door and found himself at the foot of the stairs. He wandered home still as confused as ever. He couldn't understand why Ts'ang Chieh and The Master were in such high spirits. It didn't seem like they were getting anywhere. Actually, he realized, he had no idea what they had been talking about. All he knew was the story as LiuPing was telling it which seemed to focus on Paopao and his failed ideas as much as anything else.

And, what about those rejected ideas, why did they seem somehow familiar? John felt the familiar frustration growing and then laughed at himself. "At least I'm asking questions." He shook his head in silent surrender, went home, and then spent the rest of the afternoon shopping with his family.

Nine o'clock found John up on the roof again, searching for answers, going over old ground. Focus. Of course it was important. Everyone knew that. How was that supposed to help him?

"How on earth am I supposed to focus more than I already am and on what?" he spoke into the night.

What stuck with him most was a question from earlier... Why did Paopao's ideas sound familiar? The more he thought about it the more perplexed he became. It suddenly hit him that Paopao's first two plans were actually very similar to two modern day philosophies of education. Coincidence? He suddenly wasn't entirely sure.

"This is ridiculous!" He kicked at a small dark shadow he assumed was one of the ever present pieces of rubbish. It was half a brick. He had heavy shoes on against the cold but, it hurt. In an instant the pain cleared his mind of everything else, utter focus. But it only lasted for a moment and as he limped to the railing at the edge of the roof his frustration returned twice fold.

"Did I really need that? Can't you cut me a break here? Just once?"

"Don't blame me for the frustrations you bring on yourself." The crystal clear voice rang in his head again. He stopped, looked up at another star filled sky, awed. How many of his frustrations were self-inflicted? If he could figure that out he could also then see which frustrations were there to move him... maybe he could. No, that would be even more impossible than the task already before him. Going forward however, he could try to not pile extra frustrations on himself. That might help some.

He scooped up the dog and limped down the stairs. His last fleeting thought just before entering his apartment was, "Who is this LiuPing guy anyway?"

TWELVE

Morning dawned with air so clear everything seemed to sparkle. On closer inspection John found that everything outside was indeed sparkling. Everything was once again frozen solid, every bit of moisture in the air had crystallized and settled over everything in sight as if the world had been sprinkled with crushed diamonds. It was beautiful, or as close to it as the dirty concrete city could be.

John was strangely upbeat despite his frustrations of the night before and the obvious return of sub-arctic temperatures. Today the end of the story would be told. He would have answers. Of this he was certain despite LiuPing's warning that he might not like how the story ended. There had to be a method to LiuPing's madness. No one would take this much time out of his life to tell someone a story like this and it not have answers. No one.

John arrived at the LiuPing Cafe at ten o'clock sharp. LiuPing was there, waiting, two mugs of ginger tea steaming on the table.

"So California, you are ready to hear the end of the story? I hope you're not still waiting for answers!"

"I'm still hoping you're joking about that."

"Joking, ha ha. LiuPing never joke! At least never when I'm being serious! Ha ha ha." LiuPing paused, turned serious. "So, what did you think about last night? About Paopao's first attempts? About focus?"

"To be honest, I didn't spend all that much time thinking about the attempts. The Master and Ts'ang Chieh had already rejected them and I thought their reasoning was pretty sound. It did strike me as curious though just how similar Paopao's plans were to some of the modern philosophies of education. I guess there really is nothing new under the sun."

"Similar to modern theories you say? That is curious. But what about focus California? What do you think about that?"

"I don't really know what to make of it. It's something that is given great lip service in most areas of education. But, I don't know how often we really actually do it, how often we actually focus on something intently. The current "best practices" in education have us focusing on mastery of certain measurable "standards" though many of them are only marginally measurable at best. I guess in this way you could say modern education is extremely focused. But, I'm not sure that's really true. How can it be if we're focused on measuring the immeasurable? Even if it is true, one has to ask if it's focused on the right things. That's really one of the things that drive my frustration. Our standards are not always focused on the right things so we come up with a completely separate system to somehow measure the other things that matter to us, immeasurable things like wisdom. Then we try to integrate the two systems and it just won't work. Aaagh! It's just nuts."

"Very interesting California. Shall we finish our story? I think there are parts that you may really identify with today."

"I can't wait to hear it."

"It took Paopao over a month to develop his third and final plan. In the end he was incredibly proud of it and couldn't wait to share it with

The Master and Ts'ang Chieh but he wanted to be sure it was well received. So, he waited until a day came where The Master and Ts'ang Chieh came back from a morning walk, both in the highest spirits he had ever seen them. Today, he knew, was the day. Paopao bowed before them and simply said, 'Masters, I am finished.'

For all their wisdom The Master and Ts'ang Chieh were completely unprepared for this bit of news. They assumed Paopao had given up long before. They stood looking at each other in surprise for some moments before The Master responded quite proud of Paopao's diligence.

'Paopao that is wonderful news and it couldn't have come at a better time. You see, I am planning a great feast tomorrow so we can make an announcement that will be always remembered in the history of our people. It will be a wonderful day and now, maybe your plan will be a part of it.'

Paopao beamed with pride. Could it be possible? Could he possibly have created something worthy of being remembered through the ages. He dared to dream that it might be true, that his name could even be mentioned alongside that of The Master's. It was all he had ever dreamed of, more than he'd ever hoped for. Ts'ang Chieh stared at The Master dumbfounded.

'Paopao, Master Ts'ang Chieh and I have much to discuss today. Why don't you join us this evening in my rooftop garden as before and we will listen to your new plan. Master Ts'ang Chieh, it has been an exciting morning and I need to take some rest and then I want to work on a special surprise for tomorrow night. It's something brilliantly beautiful I've been working on for some time. Tomorrow will be the perfect celebration to unveil it I think. I will meet you at our accustomed place when we both have had time to rest and eat?' The Master left Ts'ang Chieh and Paopao, still bowing, and headed to his private quarters.

'Paopao, I certainly hope you are not going to waste our time once again.' Ts'ang Chieh turned and walked off leaving Paopao still on his knees bowing.

Mid afternoon found The Master and Ts'ang Chieh sitting in the shade on the roof. Ts'ang Chieh looking at The Master curiously not wanting to ask why his arms were covered in what looked like soot and he smelled of sulfur and bat dung.

'Master, do you really think it was wise to give Paopao so much hope? We have already completed our own plan. It's not likely he will have anything that will be useful to add. This will just be yet another failure for him.'

'Ah my young friend, I understand what you are saying but, don't you think it wiser to encourage him even if we have little hope he will share anything useful? We wish for him to grow in wisdom as well do we not? I don't think it would reflect well on our own plans if we were to just cast him to the side. No, we will hear him out. Maybe he will give us something to think about, some small thing we may have missed in our own plan. To be honest, I myself am not very optimistic that he will help in any way at this point but, what can it harm to listen to him? He has indeed worked hard and I think we owe it to him to acknowledge his efforts.'

'I understand Master. You are correct of course. I'm very excited that we are ready to share our own plan and to start teaching our people what we have discovered.'

'As am I my friend. What we have created together is a truly remarkable thing. Tomorrow will be a day to be remembered; the day we changed the world. For now though, I think we have talked enough and I have more preparations to do for tomorrow's festivities. Let's meet back here this evening to hear what young Paopao has to say one last time.'

'Yes Master, I don't know what it is you are working on but I have a feeling there will be more than one surprise for the people tomorrow night!'

'Perceptive as usual my young friend. This is one surprise I'm going to keep secret even from you.'

Night came and the entire valley was aglow from the one-day-from-full moon. The river shone like polished silver in the distance. Paopao, Ts'ang Chieh, and The Master were all seated this time on the very edge of the roof gazing out across the tranquil scene. The Master ordered mugs of his special tea brought up and only after they had each been served and had savored their first mug full did he allow them to start to discus Paopao's latest plan.

'Paopao, before you begin I want to tell you how proud Master Ts'ang Chieh and I are of you. You started out as a great nuisance causing this trouble but you have worked harder and taken this more seriously than we ever dreamed you would. You have made great progress and, even if we don't decide that your plan is the best way to proceed, you should still be proud of what you have accomplished. You have done what none before have. You have designed not one but three different methods for teaching our people and I must say, though we have yet to hear the third, each has some very good merits. This is an amazing thing.'

'Thank you Master. This has been an incredibly difficult task but it is a punishment I deserved. I can only hope my penance has brought about some good. I hope that even if you decide to use nothing at all from my plans my work will have helped you and Master Ts'ang Chieh in some small way.'

'Well said young Paopao,' said Ts'ang Chieh. 'You are speaking with a maturity beyond your young years. I am looking forward to hearing your latest plan and how your thinking has grown through designing it. Please tell us, after all of your thoughts, how would you teach our people?'

'Masters, let me begin with how it is, after much thought, that I now see the learners. First, I still truly do see the people as good, yes, at the core of their beings I believe most are good and will, if allowed to discover on their own, eventually find what is right, what is true, what is wise. However, I also believe for most this is a process that takes much time, maybe an entire lifetime. Therefore I believe that it would be foolish to rely on this when trying to teach. It would be terribly inefficient and completely haphazard as my first plan was. No two students would ever learn the same things at the same time making it impossible to teach an entire group at once or to make any plans. It would also be very hard to determine if someone had actually learned anything.

My new plan relies on this innate goodness but gives guidelines for their learning and for teaching. I plan on making a complete set of guidelines for each of the things my students will learn. These guidelines will describe the skills and the facts that we want people to learn at each stage. It will be a very structured sequence of things to learn but not be a strict list of things to essentially memorize like my last plan. In this plan they will learn facts by working to master the skills described. I won't specify exactly which skills must be used to teach the individual facts. That will be left to the person teaching or, in some cases left to the individual learners. This way the learners will take an active part in discovering but they will still be very guided. It also allows the plan to have a great deal of flexibility in spite of its structure.'

'Very interesting Paopao; I can see how you are drawing on some of the strong points from your first two plans. How, may I ask, will you know if your students have learned what you wanted them to?' The Master asked.

'Well Master, I still see testing as very important. In my last plan I relied entirely on big tests at the end of periods of learning. In my new plan have changed how and when they will be tested. I have decided to first test the students before teaching them anything.'

'Why on earth would you do that?' Ts'ang Chieh interrupted. 'Testing before teaching! That sounds like a sure way for your students to fail before they even begin. They are sure to become discouraged.'

'Well Master, at first I thought the same. But, the more I thought about it, the more it made sense. You see, if I don't test them before we begin, how will I know what they already know? It may be that they already know everything about the subject I'm to teach. If I were to continue on and teach it they would look like they are wonderful learners and I am the greatest teacher. However, it would be a lie and in reality we would just be wasting time going over material they had already mastered.'

'Paopao makes a very good point Master Ts'ang Chieh,' said The Master. 'He has obviously put much thought into this plan. Please continue Paopao. What else can you tell us?'

'After the initial testing the facts and skills in the guidelines would be taught and we would stop many times to have informal little tests of different types so that I could be sure everyone was keeping up and see just how well they were progressing in their understanding of the material. Then, when we reach the end of what the guideline says to teach we would have a test so the students can show that they have mastered what is in the guidelines."

"Wait a minute. Wait a minute. Wait a minute!" John interrupted. "What's going on here? What Paopao is describing is almost exactly how we are told to teach today. You can't be telling me that our modern theory of education is four thousand years old! What's the deal? This can't be real. Are you just making all of this up?"

"Settle down California, let me finish the story and maybe it will make more sense to you." LiuPing said calmly. "Now, where was I? Oh yes, The Master was just about to ask an important question.

'Very interesting Paopao, I can see that you obviously have put much time and thought into this plan and I can see the beginning of wisdom in its design,' The Master began.

Paopao was beaming.

'However, I can see two potential problems with it and I wonder if you have thought about them and can address them for me. First, so much of your plan depends on these guidelines. How will you be able to make sure that these guidelines accurately describe just what you want your students to learn and describe it in such a way that you will be able to know when the students have learned it?'

Paopao was ready for this question as he was certain this was one of the greatest strengths of his plan.

'Master, I have taken great care in crafting my guidelines so that they clearly state exactly what mastery looks like, what the objectives for learning are. I have been able to write each one in such a way that it makes mastery of the guideline something that can be measured and tracked. It is simply wonderful.'

'If you were able to do as you say it is an amazing feat! Something even Master Ts'ang Chieh and I have been unable to do. Tell me Paopao, what about wisdom? We agreed before that wisdom must be our ultimate goal in teaching our people. Please tell me, how were you able to make wisdom measurable?'

Paopao's face fell. He knew he had failed. '

'Master, in this I have failed you. I have found no way to measure wisdom. I have even failed to find a way to teach it. Knowledge is easy. Wisdom, I don't know if it can be taught. I'm sorry I have wasted your time Masters.' Paopao hung his head in shame and got up to leave.

'Not so fast Paopao. I told you earlier that I was proud of the work you have done. That has not changed. This plan of yours, if we were only concerned with knowledge, could be a masterpiece if the guidelines are right. It is an amazing piece of work you have done, far beyond what we thought you were capable of. I think you have much more potential than we guessed and I would like to continue working with you. After we make our announcement tomorrow there will be much work to do and we will need someone like you to help us. Will you stay and continue working with Master Ts'ang Chieh and me?'

'Master, I could dream of nothing greater,' Paopao exclaimed bowing before The Masters feet.

'Wonderful! Why don't you go now and get some rest. There will be much for us to do tomorrow. Master Ts'ang Chieh and I will stay and talk just a bit longer I think.'

They sat in silence for some time after watching Paopao scurry off the roof. Ts'ang Chieh was the first to break it.

'It really was a very good bit of work Paopao did. Much better than I ever expected.'

'Yes, very impressive for one so young. We can't really fault him for having such problems focusing his plan on wisdom. It eluded the two of us for a long time also as you well know.'

'You know Master, I'm not certain that in our focus on wisdom that we ourselves didn't neglect knowledge a bit.'

'Yes, I understand what you are saying. We have created a wonderful framework for teaching wisdom. One so powerful, that in reality we could use it as a way to focus any one of Paopao's plans and they would become very useful for teaching both wisdom and knowledge. Hmmm, I think we will be working very closely with Paopao indeed. This is wonderful. Let us sleep on it and then we can discuss our plan with Paopao before the celebration tomorrow. I think he will be most happy. What a celebration it will be!"

LiuPing stopped, got up and crossed to the bar and set about starting another pot of tea. He took his time. John got up and stared out across the rooftop wondering just what it would look like in the warmth of summer. LiuPing brought John a fresh mug and stood beside him looking across the frozen scene. He smiled knowing how delightful the garden would be in full bloom. It wouldn't be long he knew but, there might be a bit more frost to endure first.

Thirteen

"So California, how did you like my story?"

"What do you mean? That can't be the end. It can't just end there. What about Ts'ang Chieh and The Master's plan? They haven't announced it yet... What was it? It sounds like it would answer so many questions!"

"Ah California, I warned you that you might not like how the story ends, that there might not be any answers that would help you. I don't know what The Master's plan was. No one does. It was lost before it could be shared."

"Lost! How is that possible? You know the story right up to the point they are going to announce their plan. How can the plan have been lost?"

"Ah, now that is a good question California. The answer won't help you at all but at least it may satisfy your curiosity. You see, the morning after Paopao presented his plan The Master asked him to come and help him with the final preparations for his big surprise. If you remember, The Master's surprise was something using sulfur, charcoal and bat dung... the basic ingredients for..."

"Gun powder!"

"Exactly California, the basic component of fireworks! Well, The Master had done a lot of experimenting but not quite enough. Paopao had listened carefully to his instructions but, in typical Paopao fashion, not quite carefully enough. The result was an explosion, an explosion so large that it leveled the entire compound and killed everyone in it, The Master, Ts'ang Chieh, and Paopao included."

"And the plan was lost."

"Yes California, the plan was lost. But, at least we have most of the story."

"But no answers. No answers at all." All of John's frustrations seemed to come to a peak at once. "So, this has all been a big waste of time? Tell me LiuPing, is this a real story or did you just make all of this up to torment me? Why tell me this?"

"Waste of time! LiuPing never waste your time. I tell you from the start that there no answers. That you need to learn to ask right questions! Never waste time."

"But, the story was so strange. The plans Paopao came up with were so like educational philosophies from the last fifty years, not four thousand. Are you sure you didn't make any of this up? You sure seem to know a lot about education. Who are you anyway?"

LiuPing smiled.

"You know John, that's probably the best question you have asked since we met." he replied, nearly all traces of his accent gone. "Who am I indeed?" This was followed with a hearty laugh. John sank back into his chair.

"What's going on here? Is this some kind of joke? What happened to your voice?"

"All good questions John. First, it's not a joke though I probably let it go on for a bit too long. As to who I am, well, if you will remember, I told you much of it when we first met." John looked thoughtful.

"You said you were some kind of businessman with two restaurants who came back to China to share what you learned in California with the people here."

"We'll that's close but I never said I was a businessman. I own two successful restaurants in California but I don't run them. I just bought them as investments when I retired. No John, what I spent much of my life doing, what I'm still doing actually, is teaching people how to teach. I'm a retired professor from a small Christian university. I came to China to help train Christian teachers here." LiuPing smiled. "That's why I knew so much about teaching and yes, some of the story was made up."

"But why?" John stammered.

"Well, at first I really thought you were going to freeze to death and foreigners always seem to trust me more when I use the accent. But, after talking to you for just a couple minutes I don't know why but I was convinced that you do actually have a story to tell. It's one I've been wanting to tell for years myself but, I haven't found the answers, or maybe haven't asked the right questions yet. I don't know. What I do know is your frustration has been leading you down a path I myself have been following for years. Your destination may be very different than mine and I wanted to help you along the way as much as I could. I know in my heart the things we have been discussing while talking about the story are pieces of the puzzle. Wisdom, questions, focus, perspective are all very important but I haven't been able to piece them together into a coherent picture. I'm hoping you have more success."

John shook his head.

"Let me see if I have this right. You are a retired professor from a Christian university who for most of his life taught people how to teach. You're now here doing the same thing but you decided to spend a huge chunk of time telling me a story that's at least partially made-up so that I can basically find the answer to something that has been your life's work because I was frustrated. Is that about it?"

"Well it sounds a bit silly when you put it that way but, yes, that is correct."

"Oh it's not silly," John laughed. "It's insane!"

"No John, I don't think it is but even if it is, doesn't matter. God often uses things man thinks are insane to bring about his purposes. Your questions and frustrations are there for a reason. God's not just doing it to torment you though it may feel like it at times. He has a plan. Do you want to know why it is that I think he is going to give you a story to tell?"

"Sure, why not."

"Ha, that's the spirit. First, let's not ignore the obvious. He moved you and your entire family half way across the globe. He doesn't just do that for fun. Second, I bet that things didn't quite feel like they fit right as soon as you got here and it hasn't gotten better with time, almost like you stepped into the wrong pair of shoes but can't take them off. Am I right?"

"Yes, that's a good way to put it."

"So, he required you to take a huge step of faith but when you did you didn't exactly land in the Promised Land right? Then, you have all of these frustrations... very specific, very focused frustrations. It's almost like he as given you a mental workout program where you have to keep going through the same frustrating exercises over and over building specific mental muscles. Muscles you are going to need to tell your story. It's much like how the Israelites had to wander the desert for 40 years. It was hardship but in the end it also strengthened them as a people in order to withstand the prolonged battle of conquering the Promised Land. In the end all of the frustration is going to be worth it because you're going to be very uniquely equipped to tell the story he is going to give you stewardship of."

"Stewardship of a story? I've never heard stewardship used that way."

"Of course stewardship! Stewardship is being responsible and making wise use of whatever it is God gives you. Why would a story he gives you to tell be any different?"

"That makes sense. I've just never thought of it that way. I understand what you are saying and I'll admit it does make some sense but, how do I deal with the frustration? I don't know how much longer I can take this, how much longer my family can."

"Well John the only thing I can say is give it back to him. If you let him carry it he will but, if you keep taking it back on yourself, well, you'd better have strong shoulders."

"This day hasn't exactly been what I had expected. The story didn't end how I expected. You aren't who I thought you were. The answers I'm getting are nowhere near what I thought they would be and, I'm as frustrated as ever but, I feel a little different somehow. Like there is hope just over the horizon. I can feel it's there but I can't quite see it yet. Strange."

"Well John, I need to leave and pack for my trip. I'll be gone for a week. I hope you will come and talk with me when I get back even if I don't have a story to tell you anymore. I'll be back next Friday."

"I will though I must say, I do kind of miss your accent," John laughed as he headed out the door.

Nighttime found John in his now accustomed place on the roof. The bitter cold of the morning had relented but a heavy foul smelling mist hung in the air obliterating any view of the night sky. John's thoughts were equally muddled. The slight hope he had felt earlier in the day, had felt since meeting that fraud LiuPing, had evaporated completely leaving him feeling utterly lost and abandoned. He broke.

"Lord, I quit. Find someone else to figure this out because I can't do it. I know you told me it's simple, that I am just missing something. I don't know what it is and you're not helping and I just don't care anymore. This is taking too much from me, from my family. We're not supposed to be this unhappy and it's my fault because I just can't leave things alone and be happy. I always have to try to fix things and... Aagh, this can't be fixed! I QUIT!!! I quit. I.... quit...."

John sighed, felt a little better, freer, fully feeling that what he had just done was right, was necessary, was good. With a quietness in his head he hadn't felt in ages he watched Pengyou run laps around the roof until exhausted. He scooped up the happy animal headed back downstairs where he surprised his wife by heading straight to bed, curling up next to her far earlier than usual. John lay there a while happily soaking in the peace and quiet. With a smile he closed his eyes to blissfully drift off to sleep. It wouldn't come. "No problem. It will come. I'm tired just not used to going to bed this early. It will come soon." It still didn't. He rolled over, fluffed up his pillow, closed his eyes. Nope.

"Get up." That crystal clear voice echoed in his head.

"No, I quit." He smiled and snuggled up closer to his wife.

"Write."

"No." He hugged his pillow squeezed his eyes tighter and tried to will himself to sleep.

"Get up."

"No!"

"Get up."

"You've got to be kidding me!" He got up, grabbed a fresh legal pad and a handful of pencils from a desk drawer and sat at their little dining room table. He stared at the blank pad. "That's exactly what my mind is," he thought, "blank."

"Write."

He started scribbling random words.

Wisdom

Standards

Questions

Focus

ESLR's

Measurable

Objectives

He looked at the list hoping to find some kind of pattern. "So many buzz words but what do they really mean?" he thought. He looked at objectives. "In LiuPing's story their objective was wisdom. What's ours?" ESLR's popped out at him. "Expected Schoolwide Learning Results." That certainly sounded like an objective to him but that one simple acronym covered a multitude of topics and was in fact one of John's major sources of frustration. The things the school listed as expected learning results were incredibly broad and completely immeasurable. "How on earth can you measure if someone is a 'lover of truth'?" John laughed. But, something about the ESLR's stuck with him. "What should our learning results be? Why are we really doing what we are?" He wrote E...S...L...R. "What else could that stand for?" He starred at it for a bit and wrote.

Every

Student

Lives

Righteously

"Not bad, certainly something to aim for," he thought. "Can I do better?"

Every

Students

Life

Redeemed

John smiled. "That's exactly what we're here for. But, how do you know if it's happened? It certainly isn't measurable." John sat staring at the paper, unconsciously doodling. One of his doodles caught his eye... a fish. "How do you know a fish is a fish?" he laughed. Interesting. "How do you know a person is a believer? What changes? What does a Christian have that a non-Christian doesn't?"

It came to him. "A Christian looks at the world differently. They have a different worldview... a Christian worldview, a Biblical worldview." But, what exactly did that mean? What does it really look like? And the biggest question, how does one get one? He added "Christian Worldview" to the list.

He then drew a line through it and wrote: "It's not measurable so it's not really relevant." He sat looking at that one word, measurable, for long moments. Why was it so important? He had no doubt that it was, but why? He realized with a start that he didn't really know other than he had always been told that it was of utmost importance. It was something that had been drummed into him when he was in the business world. All of his mentors and coaches had drilled it into him and by golly it stuck. For years he had lived with the maxim he had learned in business school "That which is measured grows." It was true. He had seen it time after time and used it to his advantage. Have an aspect of, well life, that you want to improve? Start measuring it regularly and it would grow. It was almost infallible. But why? He realized he had never even questioned it. Never even thought about it because, well, because it worked. He thought about it now.

He wrote: "What happens when you measure something?" Well, you stop and examine it closely periodically. You compare it against some standard or against itself. The simple truth of the matter suddenly hit him like a truck. "Measuring something causes you to focus on it more... that's what causes the growth. Measuring isn't important, focus is!" There really was nothing magical about it. Focus, shared focus was of utmost importance he realized. If a system wasn't focused everyone would do their own thing and the students would receive a very disjointed education.

He suddenly realized that requiring others to measure specific things was actually a very insidious, manipulative, measure of control... control over what they focused on. That really was all the standards movement in education was, a method of control to make sure teachers focused on what they were told to, and nothing else. That's why the entire movement was utterly focused on everything being measurable. It dawned on him that this approach also very consciously strove to remove anything that wasn't measurable, including such things as ethics, morality, and wisdom, from the classroom. If these things were included, it was often only as an add-on program where things had been reduced to specific, measurable, bullet points. The implications staggered him. Had he really been that controlled, manipulated, brainwashed? Was the entire system rigged? Rigged to that extent? If so, how could one escape? For that matter, could one escape at all? The simple reality was if you wanted to teach you had to follow the set rules. It was required.

"But, is it possible to follow a plan, to have a focus, that is even larger than 'the system' requires? One that will actually let you refocus the system itself?" he wrote. That's kind of what The Master's plan was... if it ever really existed. Was it possible to create a framework powerful enough that it could turn any system of education into a tool for its own purposes?

"Requiring people to all focus on the same thing isn't the problem," he wrote, "it's what is focused on that becomes the problem." The problem lies in the method of control. Making everything measurable requires you to focus entirely on cold hard facts and throw out anything that can't be neatly scored with a rubric. There is no room for the subjective. No room for opinion. No room for contradictory theories. No room for faith. We'll never inspire a student to be a "lover of truth" if we only focus on the measurable. Some things are meant to be immeasurable - though modern society may disagree. We need to be able to see beyond what modern society sees. Our focus needs to be on the immeasurable, on the infinite. Our view needs to be bigger.

He wrote: "How can we focus on things that aren't measurable?" and "How do you make someone focus on something without making them measure it and manipulatively controlling them? If he hadn't been spending so much time with LiuPing this might have stumped him. As it was, he asked these questions of himself in his mind several times, got frustrated, got distracted, scolded himself to focus, re-asked himself the questions and then laughed out loud because the answer was so simple. It was right there from the beginning. He wrote "You ask the right questions!" He was actually getting excited now. It seemed like some of the pieces of the puzzle were coming together.

John paged back over his notes. He was sure he was on the right track. His redefined ESLR was exactly what a Christian educator should be aiming for in his classes. He looked at his scratched out scribble "worldview" and the doodle of the fish. "How do you know indeed?" he laughed to himself. He was pretty sure that worldview was the key. A fully developed Christian worldview was the very definition of wisdom. He was certain that using the right questions to guide students was exactly the right approach. But, what exactly was a Christian worldview? If he could just break it down to a few core components... the things that all Christians would agree with. Leave the contentious stuff for the denominations to squabble over.

He turned to a blank sheet and wrote "worldview" right in the middle, circled it and drew one arrow from it to a blank spot on the page. He wrote "Truth". A Christian has a very different understanding of truth than a non-believer.

He drew another arrow, "Creation." This certainly is a line in the sand issue.

Another arrow, "The Fall." If creation hadn't fallen into sin there would have been no need for Jesus to come and die. There would be no Christians.

Another... "Redemption," God has a wonderful plan to restore us to himself.

And finally, "Purpose." We were created for a purpose, redeemed for a purpose and we are here now for a purpose.

John looked over the page and smiled. It was short. It was simple. Surely there were innumerable other things that helped make up a Christian worldview but, these were the essentials. "And this," he thought, "can be taught."

He yawned, and looked at the clock... 3 am. He bundled up his notes and put them in his backpack, tiptoed to his room, crawled into bed beside his wife and fell fast asleep.

The next several nights followed much the same pattern for John. First he spent hours flushing out the five areas he believed were crucial parts of a Christian worldview. He expanded them, studied them, searched for things missing. He ultimately decided that the five topics would indeed be the foundation for his model. He then, to keep it all simple, spent nearly an equal amount of time condensing that information into a series of bullet points for each topic. Then he turned to the challenge of how to help students truly develop their own world views. He knew asking the right questions was the key if the students were going to truly grow and not just puppet back what they thought they were supposed to say. He also knew he had to find a way that the questions would really set the focus of what was being learned. They couldn't just be tacked on. Ultimately, he found the answer was very closely related to how he ran his classroom and prepared his lessons already. It just needed some purposeful focusing. He couldn't wait to share with LiuPing.

Fourteen

The week passed quickly and Friday came much sooner than John thought it would. It was a bright sunny day and to John's great surprise, it was warm, spring warm. Back home he would have called it perfect shorts and a sweatshirt weather, his favorite, and it bolstered his already good mood. As he walked he noticed there were buds on many of the trees, buds that hadn't been there the day before. It amazed him how tenaciously life could flourish if it were given the smallest of chances. He was also, unfortunately, regularly hit in the face with the odor of rotting trash and of raw sewage. His world had thawed and though it wasn't all pleasant he was elated. Life was returning.

He stopped for the briefest of moments at the foot of the once foreboding but now familiar stairwell. He realized he had no idea if LiuPing would actually be there, be back from his trip. No matter, it was a beautiful day for a walk. If LiuPing was there, great, if not, well he would just walk around some more and try again another day. It was simply too nice a day and John was riding such a high from finally having answers that it would take a lot more than having to wait a day or two more to share with LiuPing to bring him down.

He found the door to the cafe unlocked and happily let himself in but LiuPing wasn't there. John looked around the cafe wondering what was going on. It wasn't like LiuPing to leave the cafe unattended. He found the door leading out onto the roof was ajar. He slid it open and stepped out into the rooftop garden for the first time. It was much larger and elaborate than he had ever dreamed looking out from inside the cafe. When in full bloom it would be amazing, paradise.

"John! You came back!" Across the roof LiuPing was wearing an apron, leather gloves and wielding a rather wicked looking pair of pruning shears. He had been pruning an arbor covered with a dangerous looking vine that had needle like thorns nearly two inches long. He dropped the shears in a bucket, pulled off the gloves and rushed across the roof to shake Johns hand. "I wasn't sure you would come back. I worried my whole vacation, worried that maybe I had gone too far, pushed too much. I wanted to call to make sure you were ok but I don't have your phone number. I was worried but, here you are and," he looked at John intently. "You look satisfied, happy even! What has happened? Have you found your answers?"

John smiled, "Even better my friend. I have found my questions! And you were right, questions are the key."

"You must tell me everything! But first, let's go inside and get something to drink. Maybe today I will use the coffee machine you have been lusting over every time you have visited. A good friend just sent me some special beans from Kona."

"That sounds amazing but actually, I think I'd rather have The Master's tea... you're going to have to show me just how to make it myself one of these days."

"You have changed since I met you John!" LiuPing laughed. "Ginger tea it is then."

"I'm not sure if I've changed or if I just feel free to be myself again for the first time in a very long time. Either way, I feel good, really good."

They went inside and as LiuPing prepared the tea John repositioned his favorite chair closer to the windows where sunlight could stream through to his sandal-clad feet. The warmth of the sun on feet that had spent far too much time in shoes far too restrictive was nearly intoxicating. A light breeze came through the open window ruffling the curtains. John sank back into the over-stuffed chair, stretched out his toes and closed his eyes. The next thing he knew LiuPing was waking him up with a gentle hand on his shoulder.

"I'm sorry John. You looked so peaceful I really didn't want to wake you but the tea is getting cold. Besides, I want to hear what you found while I was away!"

"Wow, I actually fell asleep. Hope I wasn't drooling. I haven't been getting a whole lot of sleep lately," John said with a partially suppressed yawn.

"Normally I'd think that's a sign that you're worried about something but I get the feeling that's not the case this time. What's been going on John? What's keeping you from sleeping?"

"Well, the only way I can explain it, and I'll admit it may sound a little crazy, is that God has been keeping me awake and giving me the pieces to the puzzle bit by bit." John paused and looked at LiuPing thinking for sure he would be thought insane but LiuPing just sat looking at him with a patient smile, completely nonplussed by John's revelation. He continued, "You see, the night we last met I was completely fed up. I went up on the roof and I let God have it. I told him the task was impossible. That he picked the wrong guy. I can't do this. Find someone else, I quit. I didn't pull any punches. I meant it. It felt good."

"Did it work?" LiuPing laughed.

"Ha, what do you think? Anyway, I went down to bed feeling like a great weight had been taken off my shoulders, feeling free. I snuggled up to my wife expecting to have a great night sleep but it just wouldn't happen, the voice in my head was saying write. I argued with it a lot but, in the end it was pointless to argue, I got up and started to write. By the time I went to bed early the next morning I had it. I actually had it!"

"Ah, but had what John? What is it?"

"Well, it's something different than I, than we, were looking for. In the end I had developed a new model for Christian education. No, strike that. It's not just a model for Christian education. It's for Christian educators no matter where they teach. It's a model that could allow any teacher to teach their required curriculum but to teach it to the glory of the kingdom whether they be in a private Christian school, in a public school in the states, or even in communist China."

"John, I've spent most of my career studying how to do this in a Christian school. It's incredibly difficult. You are telling me you have a model that will work not just in a Christian school but anywhere a Christian teacher finds himself? I'm not sure such a thing is even possible. What have I been missing?

"My friend, it's possible and you had most of the pieces. At least, I wouldn't have found the pieces if it weren't for your story and our conversations. Let me explain. The first revelation was a question. What do we really want the outcome of a student's education to be? We want them to be saved, to be believers. But, how do we know if it happens? Well one of your sayings stuck with me. 'How do you know a fish is a fish?' How do you know a believer is a believer? They have a Christian worldview."

"Let me stop you right there John. Worldview is one of the biggest buzzwords around right now. There are scores of books about it. There's way too much involved and, you'd never get even Christians to agree on just what it is."

"You may be right my friend but let me explain more before you dismiss my idea entirely. I think we can agree that there are fundamental differences in the way a believer and a nonbeliever look at the world. I will also agree that a complete Christian worldview has a huge number of components, many of which would be controversial even among other Christians. When it comes down to it no two people, Christian or otherwise, will ever have exactly the same worldview. However, I wondered if I could distill a Christian worldview down to its most basic components, those four or five areas of belief that are fundamental to all believers and on which they would agree. I ended up with five: truth, creation, the fall, redemption, and purpose."

"That's an interesting approach John. I'll need to think about it more before I completely buy in but I can see where you're going. Worldview is huge. I know you can see that, see the big picture. You're choosing to keep it simple. Interesting. Hmmm. Let's just assume for a moment that I agree with your worldview categories. We're still left with the big and very real question of how we teach someone. All you've done so far is define what you want them to know, to be, in the end. The big question is how are you going to get them there in a way that the learning is real and not just something that the students can simply puppet back without ever really internalizing any of it? And, how are you going to do it on top of teaching all of the normal subjects you have to teach? Isn't this going to add an additional workload onto already overworked teachers and students?"

"Great questions!" John laughed.

LiuPing sat for a full minute waiting for John to continue. John just sat drinking his tea and smiling patiently.

"Ok John, I think I'm the one getting frustrated now and you're just sitting there calmly. I don't get it. There must be more to your plan than this. What is it?"

John laughed again, "Just focus my friend." LiuPing got up and stared out the window.

"I think maybe I was too hard on you before John. Now it seems like you're playing with me. I can't say I enjoy it as much when the tables are turned like this."

"But LiuPing, I just gave you the answers." John smiled.

"Answers? Answers! All you said was that I had great questions and that I needed to focus. Those aren't answers."

"Did I? Are you sure that's what I said?"

"Ok, now you're just playing with this old man. I clearly remember you said 'great questions' and 'focus' in response to my questions."

"You're right. I did. They are the answers LiuPing and you've been telling me that all along. In order to help our students form a biblical worldview we need something, some type of lens, we can use to focus everything we do toward that end. We don't need to add all this "worldview stuff" on top of what we're already doing. We need to refocus all we're doing in such a way that it helps build worldview. How do we do this without it being something that students can just puppet back? How do we do it in such a way that it adds rigor to what we are already doing? That's easy; we don't give them the answers. We just ask great focused questions to lead them to the right answers. That's the gist of my model. It's a deliberate plan to help students develop a Christian worldview through the systematic use of structured, highly focused, open ended questions to focus lessons. Shoot, to focus an entire school if it's taken to that extent."

"I certainly understand the power of questions. We've discussed that at length. I can absolutely see how they can be used to structure a lesson. But, well, how do you go bigger than that? To focus an entire school as you say, on something as large as a worldview, even a simplified worldview, that's huge!"

"Yeah, it was pretty intimidating when it first hit me but, that's what this model is capable of. There is a lot of power in shared focus. But, I shouldn't get ahead of myself here. I haven't actually spelled out how it actually works for you yet. Let me do that and I think things will be much clearer for you."

"Can't wait to hear it."

"Ok, let me start with the biggest challenge, focusing an entire school. I think once you understand that you will easily see how it works to do the same for smaller things like a class, a unit, or even just a lesson. They are all tied together. It's really quite a simple plan. We already discussed my five categories for a Christian worldview; truth, creation, the fall, redemption, and purpose. These are of course the heart of the model.

The first step is to take each of the categories and develop one big question pertaining to it for each division of the school. These questions should be appropriate for the age of the students and they should build one upon the other. I call these Focus Questions as they are meant to be focused on school-wide. These are the kind of things that should be posted on bulletin boards and on classroom posters. They are big, big questions and they are the key to there being a shared focus on campus. However, beyond that they don't really drive what happens in the classroom. It takes a lot more than just a few big questions to form a worldview.

The next step is where my model really affects what happens in the classroom, where the real meat and potatoes of forming a worldview happens. In this step we create what I call Focused Essential Questions. These subject, unit or even lesson specific questions are sub-questions or spin offs of the Focus Questions. They are intended to help the students, with teacher guidance, start to answer the larger issues posed in the Focus Questions, to start to form their worldview. I see these questions being developed several ways. First, a school or district could create a list of sample subject specific Focused Essential Questions for each grade level. Another approach would be to have divisions in the school, ether by grade level or subject area, create questions for their respective divisions. Finally, and this is what it really comes down to, individual teachers can develop the questions themselves for their units and individual lessons. That's really where these questions come into play anyway, at the unit or lesson planning stage and in each lesson taught. These questions are intended to focus each lesson. That is, each lesson should lead a student to answer a Focused Essential Question which will help the students form answers to the larger Focus Questions.

It may help to think of the model as an organizational chart. Across the top level you have each of the five categories. Under each of these you have the Focus Questions for each of the divisions of the school. Under each Focus Question you have many Focused Essential Questions for each subject. Does that make sense?"

"I think so but let me try to sum it up to be sure. Your overall objective is for your students to be believers. No, that's not quite it, is it? You want them to be believers, who actually know what they believe, who have thought and argued through their worldviews, who are wise. You want them to be believers who could fully explain why they believe what they do and defend it. Since a complete Christian worldview is such a huge thing you have distilled it down to the essentials. You propose using big open ended questions, your Focus Questions, to keep the focus of the entire curriculum, yes, even the entire school where it belongs. Then you tie each lesson taught to one, or more, of the Focus Questions by structuring the lesson to answer some aspect of the Focus Question using what are basically follow-up questions, your Focused Essential Questions. Oh, and because you don't want your students to be puppets you probably won't provide answers for most of these question, surely never for the Focus Question. Am I close?"

"I don't think I could have summed it up better myself!" John hesitated, took a long sip of his now cold tea feeling much like he imagined Paopao must have. "So, what do you think?"

"What do I think? Well for starters, you've done an amazing job of pulling together things that are already commonly being done. For example, your Focused Essential Questions are really a modified version of the essential questions in the Understanding By Design model many teachers use. And, I've already pointed out how many people are looking at teaching worldview right now. All that aside, your model is huge while being deceivingly simple at the same time. It's a fully thought-out cohesive plan, which adds very little to a teacher's workload while adding a great deal of value, focus and purpose to what they teach. This next thing may sound like small praise but in reality it's probably the rarest thing in most curriculum plans today... it's doable, doable for every teacher, doable for any school, doable for individual teachers in non-Christian schools. John, it's what I've been looking for my entire career. In a word, I think it's brilliant!"

John simply didn't know how to respond. He just sat there with a tired lopsided grin on his face.

"There is one problem though John."

"What's that?'

"Well, we can't keep calling it 'your model.' It just won't work. Have you thought of a name for it?"

"I have actually. How about Focused by Design?"

"You know John, that just might work. Hey, I almost forgot... I thought of you on my vacation. I bought you a small gift I think is even more appropriate now." LiuPing retrieved a small red box from behind the bar. John opened it and withdrew a rectangular marble block with what looked like characters engraved in it. John looked at it curiously not sure how to react because he wasn't sure what he was looking at. He looked at LiuPing for help.

"I felt bad about the hard time I gave you and how I always called you California. It wasn't very respectful so, I gave you a proper name. That block is called a chop. It's a stamp for signing your new name... Ling De Si. Ling is your wife's maiden name so I went with it. The rest roughly means spiritual thinker. I think it's perfect."

"I, I don't know what to say. Thank you!"

"No John, I need to thank you. You have given me hope. Hope that there are still those looking to do things better than we have in the past. I am very proud of you and so glad I know you... that I got to be part of your story."

"There is one problem though LiuPing... In working on all of this I realized something. It's not just what we teach that helps students form their worldviews, it's also how we teach. This model is only part of the puzzle I'm afraid."

"Yes, I believe you are right John. How we teach may make an even bigger impact than what we teach. Hey, that reminds me of another story!"

"I'd love to hear it, but, maybe we should tell this one first?"

"As you wish John, as you wish!"

Part two

THE RATIONALE

I am not John but his story is mine. I have lived it. The frustrations that tore at him have torn at my own heart, at the hearts of my colleagues, and they have very likely torn at the heart of you my gentle reader. These frustrations tear at us because the problems we face as followers of Christ in education today, are real. They exist in every school we teach in be it a Christian school, a public school, elementary, middle, high school or college, a home school in rural America or even a prek-12th grade Christian school in a city of twelve million in communist China. They exist because we are on the front lines of a war, a war of ideologies... a war for domination of the worldview of our students. Unfortunately this is a war that we are losing on many fronts. The truth of the matter is we are outnumbered and outgunned. Our frustrations are born out of our daily battle fighting for the eternal future of our students often using inadequate, inconsistent or inappropriate tools.

Unfortunately, many in education today don't see the battle for what it is. They are content to apathetically trudge on day after day doing the same old thing they've always done, doing what they're told, believing the lies of this age... That: Information/knowledge is always good, helpful and that more is better. Organization and efficiency are some of the most important qualities in life. Technology is the key thing needed for both points above. All questions will be answered in time through science and technology, which will solve most of mankind's problems.

Truth is relative and subordinate to how one feels about information. Faith is based on believing in fairy tales. Any answers provided by religion are based on false premises thereby rendering any arguments invalid. Knowledge is equal or greater than wisdom and so on...

Others recognize the battle raging around them but are unable to effectively and consistently thwart the offensives of the enemy because they lack a clear battle plan themselves. They are able to save some who have become victims, through almost a spiritual version of triage, but they and their students are under such bombardment that they're seldom, if ever, able to take to the offensive themselves. The good news is God did not call us to have a spirit of apathy or fear but one of courage. We were meant to be courageous for such a time as this. It is time for believers to take the offensive. To do this we need to stand together with a united focus. We must have a common plan, a common goal... the salvation of our students and the renewing of their minds. But, how do we begin?

A logical place to start is looking at our purpose here as believers. Why did God put us in education at this place in this time? What is our calling? I believe the answer to these questions is pretty obvious. We are here to help others grow in faith and wisdom, to help them be transformed by Christ. This should be our primary focus. But, what does this look like? How do we know if it has happened? Ultimately it comes down to this: What do we desire the results of students being at our school to be?

As an example, a school I taught at as I was developing this model had a set of "Expected School-wide Learning Results" or ESLR's. These were supposed to paint a picture of just what/who they wanted their graduates to be.

Their ESLR's state they want their students to be:

Lovers of truth

Spiritual discerners

Versatile thinkers

Effective communicators

Mature interactors

Societal influencers

These are all good and honorable things but it is a bit hard to unpack each of the different results. It's hard to know just what this graduate would look like as the ESLR's don't paint an complete picture, but, technically, we could build a curriculum plan that would help foster each of these areas. This list of "results" looks great on a marketing brochure but in reality do they really describe just what we want our students to become? Maybe... I certainly want my students to be each of those things but I also hope for them to be so much more than that. I believe that these ESLR's are not robust enough. I don't believe they exemplify exactly what we hope our learning results to be. They don't fully express a goal.

So, what is our goal? What truly are our "Expected School-wide Learning Results?" In keeping with the acronym I put forth the following: "Every Student Lives Righteously." Now that's a pretty good goal... who really could argue against it? Even non-believers could get on board with the statement... which to me means it's still not quite strong enough. I believe the only proper, acceptable, God glorifying ESLR, the ESLR I want my own children to exemplify is this: "Every Student's Life is Redeemed." Isn't that really why we are here? Why God put us in this place in this time?

The questions then become: But how do we know if it has happened? How do we do this and still offer an excellent education? How do we do this without it becoming something the students know is tacked on and that they simply need to puppet back in order to get an "A"? The first question is the easiest to answer... if one becomes a believer their worldview will change. It will be different than that of a non-believer. What if we intentionally did all we could to help our students develop that worldview from the start?

WORLDVIEW

Every person on earth has a worldview, either Christ-centered or not, through which they view and process every aspect of the world around them. Where does it come from? Each of our students is developing their individual worldviews, what are we doing to help shape it? Each of the textbooks we use comes with a slant toward a particular worldview. Everything we do and say in the classroom affects the worldview our students will have. If we truly have the goal of our newly defined ESLR we need to help our students develop a worldview that honors God.

So, first of all, how does one develop a worldview? Where does it come from? The first and obvious way we influence our students worldview is through our direct explicit instruction. They listen to what we say, master the skills, and memorize the content we present to them. In this way we certainly have power over what they are learning but are we really influencing them? Sometimes yes, sometimes no.

Our students also, sometimes unfortunately, learn far more from our implicit teaching and actions than they do from what we purposely, explicitly say. How we teach often can leave a bigger impression on our students than what we teach. Our pedagogy is very important in forming a biblical worldview.

In the book Steppingstones to Curriculum Harro Van Brummelen describes in great detail the four prevailing philosophies of curriculum design in recent years... the traditionalist, experiential, process-mastery and Christian. It's not my intent to launch into a long drawn out examination of each in this book as it isn't necessary to understand the model for teaching I'm here to present. However, I do feel that having an understanding of these philosophies and the worldview that drives them is very important if one is going to be well versed in their profession. I will give just a very brief, very simplified, summary of these philosophies. If you'd like to delve deeper in to this area I highly recommend you pick up a copy of Harro Van Brummelen's book.

First is the traditionalist. The traditionalist philosophy is focused almost entirely on content... specifically "What are the things that the best thinkers have decided an educated person has to know?" This philosophy focuses very little on how subjects are taught, entirely ignores the nature of the learner, and relies on such "proven" strategies of "drill and kill" or rote memorization.

The next major philosophy is Process/Mastery. This philosophy is one of the most prevalent today, being the backbone of the standards movement. It, like the traditionalist philosophy, focuses on content but this focus is centered on efficiency. Content is broken down into very specific measurable pieces that are then prioritized and taught as efficiently as possible. The focus is mastery of specific measurable standards.

The experientialist philosophy has a very different focus than the first two. It instead focuses almost entirely on the learner and his/her experiences believing that we each construct our own knowledge, that each person can create their own truths, and that personal thought and experience is the most important thing.

Finally we have the Christian philosophy of curriculum. One would think that with its two thousand year old history the Christian philosophy would be the most robust and well thought out. Unfortunately this is not the case and to this point the Christian philosophy of curriculum design hasn't been clearly defined or attained widespread practice. Christian schools tend to fall into one of two camps. They are either completely focused on teaching the Bible while giving scant attention to the other content areas, relying primarily on the traditionalist model or they go the other extreme focusing on academia tacking on Bible classes and inserting a few Bible references into the secular curriculum they have adopted.

Each of these philosophies, sans the later, is firmly tied to specific, non-Biblical worldviews.

Most teachers face two major immovable roadblocks that hinder them from succeeding in guiding their students toward a biblical worldview. First, the Standards based model most schools (even private Christian schools) are currently following is firmly rooted in the process/mastery theory of curriculum. It inherently is not a Christian model of education. It reduces the students to mere objects that must live up to certain predetermined measurable benchmarks. If they don't measure up to these "objective standards" when given the standard assessment then they are failing. Secondly, the vast majority of textbooks today are written from specific secular worldviews, worldviews directly opposed to what we, as Christians, believe... the same post-modern worldviews that our students are bombarded with nearly every moment of every day.

I realize I have painted a somewhat bleak picture of our present situation but it is not without hope. We do however need to be aware of all of the challenges and we need to be educated about the competing worldviews our students are bombarded with daily. We need to have a firm understanding of how these worldviews worm there way into everyday thoughts and activities and we need to be focused on doing those things that will promote the worldview we want our students to form.

But, what is a Christian worldview?

I believe we can model a basic Christian worldview with five categories: truth, creation, the fall, redemption and purpose. Please bear in mind that the goal here is to define the most basic of Christian worldviews not one which a seminary graduate will necessarily find fulfilling... one which all believers regardless of denominational background can agree upon. This is spiritual milk... the meat and potatoes can come later. We need to first build a foundation. I will go into more detail for each of these categories below but remember... my purpose here is not to write an all-encompassing treatise on biblical worldviews. Many others have done that. We want to be able to see the big picture but keep it simple. We need something we can actually implement in our schools and classrooms not something to have endless philosophical arguments about.

Truth

- All truth comes from God. (Truth is truth. There is no secular truth apart from God.)
- We receive truth through direct and indirect revelation...
- God has provided us with a framework in which we long for and search for the truth and have the means to understand it when we find it.
- Truth is absolute and unchangeable.

Creation

- Origin--- created by God
- Carefully designed with/for a purpose
- Man was created in God's image... creative/rational/moral
- God is not part of creation... there is an eternal difference between God and man

The Fall

- Creation was warped and its nature changed.
- By nature we are against God. (sinful)
- Total depravity... we can never be good enough to gain salvation.

Redemption

- We are forgiven by grace which is freely given.
- Shows us some of the nature of God as redemption was planned from the beginning.
- Gives us hope.
- We are redeemed through the death and resurrection of Jesus, the Son of God.

Purpose

- Stewardship
- Greatest commandment
- Great commission

How do we do this?

Ok, so we have a defined purpose, our ESLR. We understand that worldview is prevalent in everything we do. We have an understanding of what makes up a basic Christian worldview. We agree that the key to reaching our ESLR goal is to be found in how we help our students form their worldviews and we agree that we want to be able to do this all the while providing an excellent education. In addition, we want to do it in such a way that it doesn't become something the students know is simply tacked on to each lesson and that they just need to puppet back without ever even thinking about it. It's an arduous task. How do we do it? The answer is actually quite simple, just one word: FOCUS. We need something that can act as a lens and refocus the activities we are already doing and the curriculum we are required to teach and transform it to the glory of the kingdom. But, what has this power? What has the power to make people focus on specific things, to think specific things? Questions of course!

In the narrative LiuPing stressed the importance of questions often. He stressed the importance of asking the right questions, the important questions. Asking questions, especially big open-ended questions, directly stimulates the mind of the listener to look for answers. Asking questions before starting any activity focuses what you will learn because your mind will be looking for the answers, often whether you want it to or not. Asking the right, focused, open-ended, leading questions will start your students down a specific path of inquiry.

Asking additional questions along the way will help them negotiate the twists and turns and keep them from chasing too many rabbit trails. Questions give you the power to guide someone along the path you wish for them to take without them feeling you are forcing them to take it and resenting you because of it. Asking good questions doesn't create puppets... it cuts their strings.

Yes, questions are the key and you can make them even more powerful if you do two things. First, write them down! The Master was right... the written word is extremely powerful. It does in fact have the power to make people think a specific thought. Written questions are even more powerful as they have the power to impel a person to ask a specific question in their minds that will start them on a path of specific thought. This is essential as someone who doesn't think about good questions, about the big questions, whose mind hasn't been agitated by them, isn't going to be ready to fully comprehend even the simplest of answers. Second, never directly give the answers to the questions... lead your students to think through the answers on their own. If they need help ask follow up questions to help them along the path. Then they won't be able to puppet back the answer they think you want to hear and they will grow in wisdom and faith.

The model I'm going to sketch out for you is one that any teacher can use in any classroom no matter where you are or what you are required to teach. However, it will be most powerful when implemented at the school level. There is great power in a group having a shared focus. That's what this model offers... a way to focus all your school does to one purpose, helping students develop their worldview.

FOCUSED BY DESIGN

The first step is to look at each of the worldview categories and create a set of "Focus Questions" for them. Focus Questions are a series of grade level appropriate questions that build sequentially upon each other and which we will answer with subject matter content in order to guide the learner in building their worldview. There should be no more than one per category per grade level or even less... per division. These are the big, hard to answer questions. The kind of questions that demand an answer long after they are first asked... almost as if they echo in one's mind. These are questions that you put up on posters on the walls of the school and everyone knows them... is focused on them.

The following are a list of sample focus questions broken down by worldview category and grade level.

Truth

Elementary: Where does truth come from?

Middle: How do we know what is true?

High: What is the nature of truth and how is it revealed to us?

Creation

Elementary: How did we get here?

Middle: How does nature reveal God?

High: How does evidence in the world show the wisdom of a grand design?

The Fall

Elementary: Why are there bad things in the world?

Middle: What does it mean to be human?

High: What are the effects of mans sin in the world?

Redemption

Elementary: How do we know God cares?

Middle: How does God show us who he is?

High: What does it mean to be redeemed?

Purpose

Elementary: How does God want you to live?

Middle: How does God want you to carry on his work?

High: How should Christians live in a world filled with suffering?

Now, I know you may be saying, "Hold on this will never work. It takes more than answering three or four questions about truth to build someone's worldview." You are absolutely correct. It will take hundreds maybe even thousands. The Focus Questions are big and hard to answer. We need a way to make them easier for our students to answer and since we want our students to grow in wisdom, and not be puppets, we can't just take the easy way out and tell them the answers. So, what do we do? We answer the questions with more questions.

I call these Focused Essential Questions. These are questions you develop while unit planning and lesson planning and which you use to guide your instruction. Essentially they are part of your objectives for the lessons. The lesson content and structure of the activity provides the means for your students to answer these questions which in turn gives them a better understanding of the Focus Question.

I have provided just a few FEQ'S below to help you understand their relation to the Focus questions. There are many more on my website www.rooftopperspectives.com

---

Subject specific
Focused Essential Questions

Truth

Elementary: Where does truth come from?

Language Arts:

•   Is this story true or make believe (fiction or non-fiction)?

•   How do you know what the author is telling you is fact or opinion?

Social Studies:

- Who should you trust?
- Did this person discover something new?
- Can the person telling this story be trusted?

Math:

- Will this fact (3+5 = 8, 4 x 6 = 24, etc.) always be true?

Science:

- How are scientific questions answered?
- What is the nature of scientific knowledge?

Middle: How do we know what is true?

Language Arts:

- How can we tell the difference between fantasy and reality?
- What is the author's purpose in writing this story?
- How does language convey meaning? How do words convey meaning?

Social Studies:

- How does ones' perspective influence their view of an event?
- What message is this media sending?

Math:

- Will this process (adding, subtracting, the distributive property, the quadratic formula, etc.) always work?

Science:

- How do we know something is true scientifically, or can we?
- Are there other ways of knowing something is true besides through science?

High: What is the nature of truth and how is it revealed to us?

Language Arts:

- Which rhetoric is used to conceal or manipulate truth?
- How is truth shown in nature, relationships, archetypes etc.?
- Is there an absolute truth? Where can truth be found?

Social Studies:

- How can one "present" truth for their own personal or national means?
- How can new findings or facts change truth?
- Can truth be bias free?

Math:

- Is mathematics discovered or invented?
- Did this concept exist (pi, irrational numbers, the Pythagorean theorem, elliptical orbits, etc.) before humans discovered it?

Science:

- Should limits be imposed on scientific investigation?
- Just because we can, should we?

The most basic summary of my Focused by Design model is this: We want to help our students develop a Christian worldview. We have distilled this worldview down to the five categories we feel are the basic non-negotiable components. We will use big open-ended Focus Questions in order to have a shared focus in our schools. We will use Focused Essential Questions to structure our daily lessons and use our curricular content to answer them.

A note to my friends teaching in public schools

Finally I'd like to say a word to my friends that are teaching in public schools. After reading all this I realize some of you may be saying, "I can't do this where I teach." You can... in fact knowing many of you already are. Sure, you are not going to be able to put posters of the Focus Questions up on your walls. Shoot, you're not even going to be able to talk about the focus questions directly but you can still use them to focus what you're teaching. You can surely still focus your daily lessons in a way that will cause your students to start asking powerful questions themselves by using Focused Essential Questions. You won't be able to quote scripture or speak directly to some of the questions your students will struggle with but you can lead them along by asking the right questions. You can and though you may not realize it... many of you already do.

AFTERWORD

I have written this book because, like John, I've felt compelled to. This is a subject that is near and dear to my heart yet at the same time one that I have wrestled with mightily. I purposely didn't write this in the conventional style of most education texts. I wanted to take you on a journey that would lead you through some specific thoughts. I wrote it in such a way as to be a conversation starter, not something that gives you all the answers. No one person has all the answers, I certainly don't, but by working together we may find them. I hope you were entertained. I hope you were challenged. I hope you have questions echoing in your head. I pray that you will start the conversation where you live and teach, that you will join the battle for our kids, that you will question everything and be blessed with discernment, that you will focus.

Will you join me in the conversation, in looking for the answers, in asking the questions, in persuading others to join us?

Will you?

Please come to www.rooftopperspectives.com.

Join the discussion and tell me what you think.

APPENDIX

Write some FEQ's yourself.

<u>Truth</u>

Elementary: Where does truth come from?

    Language Arts:

    Social Studies:

    Math:

    Science:

Middle. How do we know what is true?

    Language Arts:

    Social Studies:

    Math:

    Science:

High: What is the nature of truth and how is it revealed to us?

    Language Arts:

    Social Studies:

    Math:

    Science:

Creation

Elementary: How did we get here?

Language Arts:

Social Studies:

Math:

Science:

Middle: How does nature reveal God?

Language Arts:

Social Studies:

Math:

Science:

High: How does evidence in the world show the wisdom of a grand design?

Language Arts:

Social Studies:

Math:

Science:

The Fall

Elementary: Why are there bad things in the world?

Language Arts:

Social Studies:

Math:

Science:

Middle: What does it mean to be human?

Language Arts:

Social Studies:

Math:

Science:

High: What are the effects of mans sin in the world?

Language Arts:

Social Studies:

Math:

Science:

Redemption

Elementary: How do we know God cares?

Language Arts:

Social Studies:

Math:

Science:

Middle: How does God show us who he is?

Language Arts:

Social Studies:

Math:

Science:

High: What does it mean to be redeemed?

Language Arts:

Social Studies:

Math:

Science:

Purpose

Elementary: How does God want you to live?

Language Arts:

Social Studies:

Math:

Science:

Middle: How does God want you to carry on his work?

Language Arts:

Social Studies:

Math:

Science:

High: How should Christians live in a world filled with suffering?

Language Arts:

Social Studies:

Math:

Science:

Unit plan, lesson plan, and FEQ templates and more available at: www.rooftopperspectives.com

THE AUTHOR

Eric Reenders
For more information please join me at:
www.rooftopperspectives.com